D1453577

The Scots Philosophical Monograph Series

While this monograph series is published on behalf of the Scots Philosophical Club, refereed by a panel of distinguished philosophers in the Club, and has as one of its aims the provision of a publishing outlet for philosophical work being done in Scotland, it is nevertheless international. The Club is committed to bringing out original works, written in a lively and readable style, and devoted to central areas of current philosophical concern, from philosophers working anywhere in the world.

As a deliberate policy we have specified no areas of the subject on which the series is to concentrate. The emphasis is on originality rather than, say, on surveys of literature, commentaries on the work of others, or exegesis. Historical works are included only in so far as they also contribute significantly to topical debates.

As well as our debt to the referees and consulting editors, we have to acknowledge a very real debt to the universities of Glasgow, Edinburgh, Aberdeen, Stirling and St Andrews who—despite the current stringencies—have given financial support to the series.

Series Editors: Andrew Brennan, William Lyons

Consulting Editors:
J R Cameron *Aberdeen*
Neil Cooper *Dundee*
Robin Downie *Glasgow*
R W Hepburn *Edinburgh*
Bernard Mayo *St Andrews*
Neil Tennant *Stirling*
Crispin Wright *St Andrews*

Scots Philosophical Monographs Number Six

THE RANGE OF
EPISTEMIC LOGIC

Scots Philosophical Monographs

Scots Philosophical Monographs Number Six

THE RANGE OF
EPISTEMIC LOGIC
GEORGE N SCHLESINGER

Series Editors Andrew Brennan & William Lyons

ABERDEEN UNIVERSITY PRESS
HUMANITIES PRESS: NEW JERSEY

BC
71
$.S427$
1985

$Cop.2$

First published 1985
Aberdeen University Press
A member of the Pergamon Group

© George N Schlesinger 1985

British Library Cataloguing in Publication Data

Schlesinger, George N.
   The range of epistemic logic. — (Scots
   philosophical monographs, ISSN 0144–3062; no. 6)
   I. Title   II. Series
   160   B945.S3/

ISBN 0–08–032416–9
ISBN 0–08–032417–7 Pbk

PRINTED IN GREAT BRITAIN AT
ABERDEEN UNIVERSITY PRESS

Contents

7 BELIEF AND UNDERSTANDING

8 THE VERIFICATION THEORY OF MEANING

Preface

Approximately one third of the book's material is based on papers published in the *Australasian Journal of Philosophy Erkentniss* and the *Philosophical Studies*. I wish to thank the editors for permitting me to use their journals as sounding boards for some of my ideas.

This is a welcome opportunity to put on record my appreciation of some of those I have had the good fortune to exchange ideas with, to be instructed and intellectually stimulated by, over the years. These include: Maynard Adams, a philosopher in the truest sense; a lover of wisdom and a compassionate and judicious friend and teacher; Doug Long and Bob Vance whose shrewd critical comments I have invariably found illuminating; Bruce Waller, a paragon of patience, good will and good sense; David Zelicovici, the most popular and effective teacher of philosophy I have ever known whose mind is always overflowing with novel ideas.

I should also like to mention two of our graduate students, B M Goodman and J P Coley who on several occasions spotted and corrected my stylistic errors.

Finally I should like to pay a deeply felt tribute to the late Yishai Davidi, a unique individual greatly admired for his uncompromising integrity, much of whose life was dedicated to working selflessly for the welfare of others.

Introduction

All of us like ventures where the returns are disproportionately high relative to the initial investment. Elementary epistemic logic is simple to the point of triviality and may be mastered without great effort but it turns out to be a versatile tool readily yielding a great many useful results. This is its great attraction. Most of us are fascinated upon seeing mighty things from small beginnings grow, and delight in simple things that are capable of accomplishing more than their more cumbersome alternatives. In this spirit we can observe with interest the varied services this fairly novel branch of formal logic may perform.

In general, the introduction of formal methods into philosophy during this century has had the greatest transforming effect upon the discipline. It has radically improved clarity of expression and rigour of argumentation. However, it has not met with unqualified enthusiasm everywhere. There are highly intelligent people lacking a special mathematical aptitude who have found a variety of matters to complain about.

Some maintain that the use of formal techniques, instead of increasing clarity, often leads to the very opposite, namely the weaving of such entangled webs around a basically straightforward and simple idea as to make it penetrable only to those who are specially skilled in cutting through dense formal thickets. Hao Wang, a first rate practitioner of formal techniques has nevertheless acknowledged that these 'often give the impression that a formidable technical book expresses in tiresome exactitude more or less commonplace ideas which could be conveyed more easily and more directly in a few sentences of plain language'. Some have gone even further to charge that trivial issues are often made to look more impressive when blown up by formal contrivances to a size much in excess of their real importance.

Another undesirable product of the wholesale mathematisation of our discipline, others complain, has been the blurring of the boundaries between philosophy and areas of knowledge that are definitely not philosophy. Since the methodology of philosophy has come to resemble the methodology of the strictly mathematical and natural sciences it is much easier to overlook the fact that some works purporting to deal with philosophy are essentially dealing with linguistics, mathematical logic, foundations of mathematics, probability theory and statistics, decision theory, theoretical physics and so on.

Undoubtedly such charges have more than a grain of truth in them. However, it would be a great pity to allow oneself to overlook the overwhelmingly many positive aspects of formal methods. At this moment there may be nothing more suitable to dramatise the versatility, efficiency and clarifying power of formal techniques when put to work in philosophy than elementary epistemic logic.

By elementary epistemic logic I refer only to those basic techniques which do not require us to enter into the problems associated with quantifying into epistemic contexts and to deal with the difficulties of having to distinguish between *de dicto* and *de re* sentences.[1] In other words we will deal with an elementary system which presupposes practically nothing more than a beginners course in symbolic logic. The reader should soon discover to his astonishment that in this particular area of applied logic a tiny bit can go very far. He may be assured that he will not be confronted with anything impenetrable or with any formal manoeuvring the purpose of which is not entirely transparent. Because of the brevity and elementary nature of the formal arguments to be employed, there will be no possible grounds for complaints that have been characteristically made against the unbridled use of formal techniques in philosophy.

In the coming chapters we shall look at many issues: the way epistemic logic may be used to lay bare the precise structure of reasonings that have hitherto been accepted without close scrutiny because of their intuitive appeal, the manner in which the full nature of familiar concepts may be explicated through providing a rigorous formal definition, and the method whereby the covert presuppositions underlying certain epistemic theses and their hidden logical relations to other theses may be brought to the surface. I shall attempt to reveal the many faceted nature of epistemic concepts by highlighting their far reaching ramifications impinging upon such concepts as 'understanding' and 'meaningfulness'.

Probably the most unexpected feature of our topic is to be found in Chapter Six where it is demonstrated that all the various difficulties, puzzles and paradoxes that have hampered the development of deontic logic can smoothly be resolved once we realise that the two branches of applied logic—namely the logic of obligations and that of knowledge—are precise replicas of one another.

The last two chapters deal with the fundamental distinction between two kinds of implications: content-dependent and content-independent

---

[1] Notes start on p. 111.

implications. In a sense this topic is more important than that of Chapter Six because of its far wider ramifications. The reason why the crucial distinction is so little known is that it plays no role in pure logic. However, it has great many uses in applied logic. This will be illustrated in Chapters Seven and Eight through a number of examples of the exceedingly important results obtainable by making use of this distinction.

1

Is There an Epistemic Logic?

Section 1
The problem

It seems appropriate to begin a work concerning the many uses of epistemic logic by setting out to tackle the challenge posed some time ago in an important paper by Max Hocutt in which he questions the existence of such a thing as epistemic logic.[1] Admittedly there exist logical relations like

$$Ksp \rightarrow p \quad \text{(if } s \text{ knows that } p \text{ then } p \text{ is true)}$$

$$Ksp \rightarrow Bsp \quad \text{(if } s \text{ knows that } p \text{ then } s \text{ believes that } p\text{)}.$$

The truth of these expressions however follows directly from the definition of 'knowledge' which has traditionally been 'justified, true belief'. After all it is also the case that 'i is a bat' logically implies 'i is a mammal' as well as 'i can fly' by virtue of the definition of 'bat' as a 'flying mammal'. Yet we do not speak of a chiropteric logic, a logic specially dealing with bats.

Now of course the expression $Bsp \ \& \ (Bsp \supset Bsq) \rightarrow Bsq$ is true and its truth does not follow from any definition but it is no more than an instance of plain *Modus Ponens*; epistemic terms do not occur in this expression essentially. It should be different with

$$[Bsp \ \& \ (p \rightarrow q)] \rightarrow Bsq$$

(i.e. if s believes that p and as a matter of fact q follows from p, then it is inevitably the case that s also believes that q) which is not a case of *Modus Ponens*. However, the trouble with the last expression is that there are no grounds on which to maintain it to be a theorem.

Section 2

A theorem of epistemic logic

In this chapter we shall take the first step toward demonstrating the existence of epistemic logic as well as illustrate the unique, valuable function it may fulfill. We shall see that unquestionably there are statements expressing logical truth in which epistemic terms occur essentially, and some of these may be employed to establish results we could otherwise not establish.

On first thought it may appear that

$$(a) \quad [(p \rightarrow q) \mathbin{\&} JBsp] \rightarrow JBsq$$

(where '$JBsp$' stands for 's is justified in believing that p') is a good example of a statement in which epistemic terms appear essentially, and is true. After all, unlike Bsq, the question whether $JBsq$ holds does not seem to depend on s's logical acumen or state of mind. Even if s fails actually to grasp the connection between p and q, since objectively speaking q is 'included' logically in p which s is justified in believing, there would seem no reason to deny (a).

Admittedly (a) has been denied recently, but I believe on the basis of faulty argument. Steven Levy questions the validity of

$$(b) \quad [Ksp \mathbin{\&} (p \rightarrow q)] \rightarrow RBsq$$

where $RBsq$ stands for 'it is rational for s to believe that q'. He says:[2]

> Suppose that s knows that p, that p entails q and that s correctly infers q from p. We may, perhaps, be tempted to approve that any belief formed by S that q, as a result of this process is a rational belief without inquiring further into the matter. But to do so would be a mistake. Suppose that s also has a firm belief that r (it makes no difference whether or not this belief is rational). Suppose further, that r entails not $-q$ and that S correctly infers not $-q$ from r. In such a situation it would hardly be rational of s to believe that q. Rather, s should be required to escape the dilemma either by further inquiry or by suspending any belief that q or not $-q$. Thus, even though the antecedent of (b) is satisfied, given s's other beliefs it would not be rational for him to believe q.

This argument is erroneous. After all there are two possibilities:

(1) r is not sufficiently well established. Thus in view of the fact that p, which is known by s to entail q is strongly enough supported, s is in fact not justified in holding r (which he has correctly inferred as being inconsistent with q).

(2) s is objectively justified in continuing to subscribe to r since r has been firmly enough established.

Now in case (1), s either adopts the attitude that is required by the standards of rationality or he does not. Should he choose the first alternative there is certainly no problem; s in *fact* rejects r and can therefore hold q without any reservations. Undoubtedly therefore we may insist that the consequent of (*b*) is as true as its antecedent. Should he adopt the second attitude, (*b*) still remains true since now the antecedent, and not only the consequent is false! Given that s believes r and thus $\sim q$ and assuming that he knows that $\sim q \to \sim p$, it follows that $\sim Bsq$ and thus $\sim Bsp$, hence $\sim Ksp$.

In case (2) of course it follows that q has to be withdrawn because of its incompatibility with the well established r. Thus it can no longer be the case that $RBsq$ nor that $RBsp$ and therefore $\sim Ksp$. Once more therefore (*b*) remains true since its antecedent is false.

To summarise: Levy's example is harmless, since no matter what the circumstances are, either $RBsq$ remains true, or if not, Ksp is false too.

However, (*a*) may be rejected on other, legitimate grounds. Many philosophers hold that s is not justified in believing that p even if p can be established on the basis of what s knows, as long as s himself is not aware of the way this is to be done. Suppose that Goldbach's conjecture is true and I believe this to be so and there exists a rigorous proof showing this to be so; however I am ignorant of this proof and have not been assured of the truth of Goldbach's conjecture by any expert who is familiar with the proof. Then I can neither be said to know that Goldbach's conjecture is true nor that I am justified in believing this to be so. In other words, the question whether $JBsp$ is true or false is not determined solely by such objective factors as the evidence s possesses and the logical relationship between it and p. Admittedly it is a necessary condition that there be adequate evidence but unless s also realised this, $JBsp$ is not true.

Let me therefore introduce the symbol JB^*sp to mean 'objectively speaking, it is rational to accept p on the basis of information in s's possession', which of course, amounts to less than $JBsp$ (which stands for 's is actually justified in believing that p'). JB^*sp may be true when $JBsp$ is false as when s himself is not aware of the relevance of the evidence he possesses and cannot see that it justifies a belief in p. It may seem then that

$$(c) \quad [(p \to q) \ \& \ JBsp] \to JB^*sq$$

represents a logical truth. It turns out however that even (*c*) will not do. Suppose that s has adequate evidence that p is true and thus $JBsp$, even though in fact p is false. Also suppose that s is incapable of inferring q from p

but can clearly see that q is false. In this case JB^*sq is false in spite of the fact that the antecedent of (c) is true.[3]

However (c) may be amended in a number of ways to yield a valid expression. It is possible for instance to substitute 'K' for 'JB' and obtain

$$(d_1) \quad [(p \to q) \;\&\; Ksp] \to JB^*sq.$$

The previous objection does not apply to (d_1) since no longer can p be false given that s knows that p. Now (d_1) is not of much use because when we find its antecedent true then though we are entitled to assert the consequent, JB^*sq, this has no practical significance. It does not matter who is named by s, since even the best flesh and blood individual cannot be depended on not to have occasional mental blocks and thus fail to make even the most obvious inference. $JBsq$ does not necessarily follow from JB^*sq.

However (d_1) is logically equivalent to

$$(d_2) \quad [(p \to q) \;\&\; \sim JB^*sq] \to \sim Ksp.$$

The last expression is useful and I propose to provide an important illustration of its application.

Section 3

The reconstruction of Descartes's dream argument

Mark Steiner in discussing Descartes' dream Argument[4] points out that the premises with which Descartes starts out are:

$(p_1) \quad \sim K \sim D \quad$ (I do not know that I am not dreaming)

and

$(p_2) \quad D \to \sim KS \quad$ (If I am dreaming I do not know that I am standing up)

and his conclusion is

$$(g) \quad \sim KS.$$

Now since Descartes has not asserted that D it is not clear how (g) may be derived from (p_1) and (p_2). Steiner claims that (g) may be derived from the given premises provided we add a third premise not mentioned by Descartes, namely:

(*)   If one is committed to $\sim KP$ (for any sentence, P) then it is irrational for him to assert P.

His demonstration then proceeds as follows:

(1)	$KS \rightarrow \sim D$	from (p_2) by contraposition
(2)	$K(KS \rightarrow \sim D)$	(1) Necessitation Rule of Epistemic Logic
(3)	$KKS \rightarrow K \sim D$	(2) Another rule of Epistemic Logic
(4)	$\sim K \sim D \rightarrow \sim KKS$	(3) Contraposition
(5)	$\sim KKS$	(p_1) and (4) *Modus Poneus*
(6)	Asserting KS is irrational	(5) and(*)

Before examining critically this ingenious suggestion let us note that the brief derivation happens to contain at least one theorem that is special to epistemic logic as well as a unique rule of inference.

The theorem is, of course, the third premise (*). Premise (*) certainly sounds reasonable yet it is by no means clear that it could be established as resulting directly from the definition of 'knowledge'.

The rule of inference Steiner has been using in taking Step 2 may be stated as:

(REP)   If in the course of his reasoning *a* arrives at the expression ϕ then *a* is entitled to assert that $Ka\phi$.

This rule may well be claimed to follow from the definition of 'knowledge' alone:

(i)   Since ϕ follows logically from the premises, ϕ is true.

(ii)   Since it is *a* who has derived ϕ surely he must have thought that his derivation was legitimate and thus $Ba\phi$.

(iii)   Since the derivation is indeed valid, $JBa\phi$.

Yet these are good grounds for regarding *REP* as a characteristic rule of epistemic logic. *REP* is certainly not trivial in the sense that if we construct any logic based on the definition of any concept we shall inevitably end up with a rule of inference that is a counterpart of *REP*. *REP* is unique to epistemic logic; it is because the conducting of logical reasoning itself requires knowledge that *REP* becomes available in that logic.

Section 4

Criticism of the reconstruction

As I have said Steiner's reconstruction is ingenious. In fact too much so, thus it is hard to believe that Descartes 'thought' of all this in the vaguest sense of that term. I believe that many will have a strong feeling that there must be some other, shorter way, by which to arrive at (6). Let me supply an argument showing why this feeling is justified.

We shall suppose that there are two surveyors a and b where a is a highly intelligent person who among other things is an accomplished logician while b is a very simple minded person whose numerous limitations include a total ignorance of formal logic.

CASE 1   Take Da: The calculator used by a is defective

S: The amount of material required to cover the walls of building B is n.

Let us also suppose that a performs a series of measurements and computations some of which he checks with his calculator and at the end of which he arrives at the conclusion that S—which happens to be true. It so happens that a does not know (while b does know) that the computer he is using was not defective. It is clear then that we have

$$(p_1')\quad \sim Ka \sim Da \quad \text{and} \quad (p_2')\quad Da \to \sim KaS.$$

These being parallel statements to those dealt with by Steiner, we need not go into details in order to show that a will arrive via the steps taken by Steiner at (5') $\sim KaKaS$.

CASE 2   Let us have the previous situation repeated exactly while substituting b for a and vice versa. In particular b is now using a calculator which *he* does not know to be in good order, while a knows this (and soon the role of this bit of assumption will become clear). Obviously we shall get as far as (1'') $KbS \to \sim Db$, but no further. Steiner has explained that he moved from (1) to (2) $(= K(1))$, on the assumption that if I myself have demonstrated the truth of (1) then surely not only must (1) be true and I believe it to be true, but I am justified in believing it to be true, that is, I know that (1) is true i.e. $K(1)$. Thus the move from (1) to (2) is facilitated not by pure logic alone, it also requires that I myself should have derived (1) from true premises, that is from (p_2). It follows therefore that for any person who is not aware that (p_2) entails (1) because, for instance, he does not know the rule of logic called contraposition, and b is such a person, $K(1)$ is not true and hence (6) remains underivable. In other words it is impossible to demonstrate that $\sim KbKbS$.

Some may find this result paradoxical. We have seen that a who is a superior surveyor does definitely not know that S, while b, in spite of the fact that he is much less likely to do a good job, is in the advantageous position in which he cannot legitimately be labelled as being ignorant of his knowledge that S. There will however be philosophers who will not find this result intolerable. In other contexts it has already been remarked that sometimes 'One may know less by knowing more'[5] and it is not ultimately strange that a sophisticated person should be shrewd enough to discern certain obstacles that stand in the way of knowing a proposition which may happen to be true, obstacles to which a more simple minded person remains oblivious. Hence the former may gain the insight to conclude that he is not entitled rationally to subscribe to S even though S may well be true while another person in his blissful ignorance cannot be disqualified from holding that he knows that S. It was after all Socrates who said that he knew more than others since he was aware of his total ignorance. It may well be that Socrates happened to hold a lot of true beliefs, beliefs also held by his fellow Athenians. Yet he, but not they, disowned the claim that he actually knew that those beliefs represented the truth.

However from our previous story we may also derive another strange looking result which cannot so easily be smoothed out. While admittedly $Kb(KbS \rightarrow \sim Db)$ does not follow from (1″) the expression (2*) $Ka(KbSb \rightarrow \sim Db)$ is derivable since a knows enough logic to arrive at (1″). From this, following Steiner we get

$$(3^*) \quad KaKbS \rightarrow Ka \sim Db$$

which is the counterpart of (3) and

$$(4^*) \quad \sim Ka \sim Db \rightarrow \sim KaKbS$$

the counterpart of (4). We recall that in the original reasoning Steiner's next step was to apply *Modus Ponens* to (p_1) and (4) to derive

$$(5) \quad \sim KKS.$$

It is however, clearly impossible to make the parallel step here to derive from $(p_1{}^*)$ and (4*)

$$(5^*) \quad \sim KaKbS$$

since $(p_1{}^*)$ is $\sim Kb \sim Db$ and the antecedent of (4*) is quite a different proposition, namely, $\sim Ka \sim Db$. Not only are we not given this last proposition but in fact it was explicitly stipulated that on the contrary $Ka \sim Db$ for we said that a knew that the calculator used by b was in working order.

We have thus reached a paradoxical result. We have seen that in Case 1 a definitely does not know that KaS but in Case 2, which is a mirror image of Case 1 with the roles of a and b precisely reversed, a *himself* in spite of all his knowledge and intelligence is not in the position to declare b to be ignorant of KbS or that b is ignorant of KbS. The previous explanation does not seem to be applicable here. After all Socrates who was enlightened enough to

hold that he knew nothing, did not regard his intellectually less accomplished fellow citizens to be more knowledgeable. On the contrary he
was prepared to declare their ignorance even with greater conviction than
his own.

Thus we have added reason to believe that there exists a different
derivation of Descartes' conclusion, in particular, one which is more
straightforward and does not require the troublesome step from (1) to (2),
which is not legitimate, unless the knower himself has established (1). We
expect there to be a briefer route leading to the conclusion one which will
also permit the derivation of $\sim KaKbS$ no less than $\sim KaKaS$.

Section 5

The application of the theorem

In my book *Metaphysics: Methods and Problems*, I have demonstrated that
by applying elementary probability notions, Descartes' conclusion may
easily be derived from (p_1) and (p_2). It seems to me now however that Steiner
would be entitled to reject this derivation. He may very well claim that it is a
misunderstanding of the concept of probability to think that it may be
applied in the context of Descartes' argument. We are certainly not faced
with a situation concerning which we could say that in the past in similar
instances the frequency of cases that turned out to be such that our
experiences have proved to have been generated by genuine external factors
was such and such. It makes therefore no sense to assign any probabilities
to metaphysical statements in general and to the statement 'the external
world exists' in particular.

However, we are now in a position to overcome all difficulties and
objections by making use of the epistemic principle we introduced in section
two, namely

$$(d_2)\quad ((p \to q)\ \&\ \sim JB^*aq) \to\ \sim Kap.$$

Descartes asserted (p_1) $\sim K \sim D$. The reason he gives is that all his
experiences are insufficient to imply, indicate or provide rational basis for
believing with enough confidence that was what goes on in his mind is
generated by corresponding external factors any more than this is true in
the case of a dream. In other words he holds $(p_1{}^*)$ $\sim JB^* \sim D$. Now
substitute into (d_2) KS for p and $\sim D$ for q and we get

$$(d_2{}^*)\quad ((KS \to\ \sim D)\ \&\ \sim JB^* \sim D) \to\ \sim KKS.$$

Conjoining (1) and $(p_1{}^*)$ we get the antecedent of $(d_2{}^*)$ and that together
with $(d_2{}^*)$ logically implies by *Modus Ponens* $\sim KKS$.

With the aid of our theorem we thus are able to derive quickly the desired conclusion without having to make use of concepts like probability whose applicability in the present context may be questionable. The brevity of our proof in comparison to Steiner's makes it into a somewhat more likely candidate to be a reconstruction of Descartes' own reasoning. An additional important advantage it has of course is that it does not involve Steiner's problematic move from (1) to (2) and our proof is therefore independent of the logical acumen of the knower.

2

The Logic of Avowals of Inner Experiences

Section 1

The varieties of privileged access

Many philosophers would agree that when the set of propositions constituting our universe of discourse consists exclusively of propositions describing one's current mental state then there are a number of theorems that are unique to epistemic logic.

One of the well known theses concerning this special kind of propositions is the Incorrigibility Thesis. According to it, necessarily if a has not misspoken and honestly says that he has an itch or a pain; that he has a pleasant taste in his mouth; that he feels tired, hot, cold or wet or in general that he has a certain sensation or awareness, then he has it. Frequently the thesis has been formulated not in terms of utterances but in terms of beliefs, i.e. 'Necessarily, if one believes he has a certain sensation or awareness, then he has it.' William Alston calls it the Principle of Infallibility.[1] In symbols:

$$(P1) \quad Bap \to p$$

(where p ranges over propositions describing a's current mental state).

Another principle Alston advances is that of Omniscience which states that a person is never ignorant of his occurrent mental states. In symbols:

$$(P2) \quad p \to Bap$$

i.e. if a has a certain sensation etc. then of necessity he believes he has it.

In this section I am not going to inquire which, if any, of the variety of theses relating to privileged access is correct and why. Such an inquiry would mostly require probing into the nature of the mind and thus belong to philosophical psychology more than to the theory of knowledge. In any case formal epistemic logic is not likely to be found very serviceable a tool in such an enterprise. My main objective will be to discover some of the presuppositions and implications of the commonly known theses that have been advanced concerning mental statements and raise questions about the logical relations existing among them.

One such question one may wish to raise at this point is whether (*P2*) must be postulated separately and whether it could not be derived from (*P1*)? We shall take it as given that whenever p is a statement describing a's mental state then so is $\sim p$. We then have from (*P1*):

(1a) $Ba \sim p \rightarrow \sim p$ and from this we get by Transposition
(1b) $p \rightarrow \sim Ba \sim p$

which asserts only that a does not positively believe that $\sim p$ and that is compatible with a at the same time not believing p either. In other words the possibility that $\sim Bap$ & $\sim Ba \sim p$ (for short, Wap, meaning 'a withholds belief concerning p') be the case has not been ruled out.

It is worth noticing however, that (*P1*) does entail that it is in principle impossible for a person to hold inconsistent beliefs about his mental states. Let us recall that if q denotes a non-mental statement then (α) Baq & $Ba \sim q$ is in the view of many philosophers not strictly speaking a contradiction. While it may as a matter of psychological law be an impossibility that (α) be instantiated by any human subject, logic has nothing to say about its truth-value. Suppose now once more that p is restricted to statements of first person mental state beliefs. In this case of course it follows that if we were to assume (α') Bap & $Ba \sim p$ to be true, then by conjoining it with (*P1*) and (1a), by *Modus Ponens* we get p & $\sim p$, which is a contradiction. Hence (α') *is* logically impossible.

A parallel question we may consider is, whether the claim that a certain person believes himself to be mistakenly subscribing to a given proposition, is coherent? At first glance it may very well seem that it is an incoherent claim. After all, a's contention is that it is a mistake for him to believe that q although as a matter of fact he does hold q to be true. But if I explicitly maintain that holding q is a mistake then that amounts to my repudiation of q i.e. it amounts to an expression of disbelief that q is true. But once it has been clearly stated that I disbelieve that q it can no longer be consistently maintained that I do believe it. Thus the claim in question is self-contradictory.

However, when we examine the matter formally we see that this is not so. The claim in question may clearly be symbolized as $BaMaq$ which by the definition of M amounts to $Ba(Baq$ & $\sim q)$ i.e. $BaBaq$ & $Ba \sim q$. Now before it will be possible for us to continue it will be necessary that we agree that $BaBaq \rightarrow Baq$. That this implication holds should be obvious enough on the view that to have a belief means to have a certain attitude of mind which is essentially to be in a mental state. For in that case it follows that Baq—regardless of what q itself may be—is a statement describing a's mental state and thus belongs to the universe of discourse members of which obey (*P1*). Therefore it seems that the claim which on an informal analysis looked self-contradictory, yields no real contradiction since as we have explained earlier, as long as q stands for a non-mental statement, the expression Baq & $Ba \sim q$ would be regarded by many not to constitute a formal contradiction.

Let me pause here a moment and try to explain how it is that a convincing—albeit informal—argument can indicate that a certain expression is self-contradictory while we subsequently show it is not. The answer is that our first argument, because of a lack of precision to which informal arguments are typically vulnerable, yielded an unwarranted result. If we look at it more carefully it should become evident that all that the first argument has shown was that a would both repudiate and embrace q. This however merely means that he would be holding inconsistent beliefs since to repudiate q amounts to subscribing to $\sim q$ while to embrace it amounts to subscribing to q. As we have seen, however, to ascribe inconsistent beliefs to a i.e. to claim that Baq & $Ba \sim q$ does not involve a contradiction.

On the other hand, of course, in the context of p-like statements, since it has been shown that (α') does amount to a contradiction, our conclusion must be different. We have to say that it follows from (*P1*) that unlike in the case of other propositions, in the case of avowals of one's own experiences it is logically false that a certain person believes himself to be mistakenly subscribing to a given proposition.

It will be of interest to look very briefly at an alternative view which interprets belief behaviouristically. According to this view, whose chief spokesman has been G Ryle, a belief is essentially a disposition.[2] Thus to say that Baq, is to say that if the circumstances were such-and-such then a would act in a certain way or say certain things. The question arises then : is the formula $BaBaq \rightarrow Baq$ valid on this view as well? In order to answer this question we have to inquire precisely how these philosophers would interpret the expression $BaBaq$? To say that it means 'a has the disposition to have the disposition to perform A_q' is probably wrong since the disposition associated with beliefs is always toward either an act or an uttering and not toward the having of some disposition. It is plausible to suggest that $BaBaq$ means 'a has the disposition to utter an honest affirmation (on appropriate occasions) that Baq'. Clearly, however, if a's affirmation that Baq is properly described as honest then Baq is true. Thus $BaBaq$ is true on this view too.

It is noted that (*P2*) on its own entails a principle we may represent by (*P3*) $\sim Wap$ i.e. a never withholds judgement with respect to any proposition describing his mental state. It may be derived formally in a few steps. It follows from (*P2*) by

Transposition: (2a) $\sim Bap \to \sim p$ Now substituting $\sim p/p$ into (*P2*):
                 (2b) $\sim p \to Ba \sim p$ and from this by contraposition:
                 (2c) $\sim Ba \sim p \to p$

Conjoining (2a) and (2c) yields $(\sim Bap \,\&\, \sim Ba \sim p) \to (p \,\&\, \sim p)$. Thus by reduction:

$$\sim(\sim Bap \,\&\, \sim Ba \sim p) \text{ (i.e. } \sim Wap) \text{ Q.E.D.}$$

Let me emphasise that (*P3*) cannot be said to follow 'trivially' from (*P2*). Admittedly Alston does not mention (*P3*) as a principle separate from (*P2*) and one might easily come to believe that it is already included in (*P2*). After all the assertion that if p then Bap applies to every p; thus whether p affirms the presence or the absence of a certain sensation, once p is given Bap must be assumed to be true. But a specific sensation is either present or is not, hence what room is left there for any occasion on which a might be withholding judgement? This argument however is based on the tacit assumption that whenever p is a statement describing a mental state then so is $\sim p$. This may be quite true but it certainly does not follow from logic alone. To use an illustration from a neighbouring area: assuming that there are such things as observation statements, then if o denoted the statement 'There is a green circular spot somewhere on the Great Wall of China on 15 May 1984' it should qualify as an observation statement since its truth can be ascertained by any normal person directly by looking at that spot. Surely, however, $\sim o$ is not an observation statement.

Even if it were claimed that it is within practical possibility that a single individual should establish with complete certainty that he has inspected every part of the Wall he would have to rely on his memory and since his inspection would have to last more than a day he would be unable to know that on 15 May there was no such spot at one end of the Wall while he was examining the other end. It might therefore not be quite absurd to imagine that ascertaining that I have no pain at all at time t (that is, ascertaining that I have no pain in any one of my 32 teeth, in any one of my 10 fingers etc.) cannot be done without the help of memory and thus it is a basically different state of affairs from when I do have a pain that is immediately presented to my awareness.

An important question to ask now is: can one not derive (*P1*) from (*P2*) by logic alone? The answer is that we could, provided the truth of (α') $Bap \,\&\, Ba \sim p$ was granted. We have however mentioned earlier that the existence of certain people—whom Hocutt calls Logically Obtuse Men[3]—cannot be ruled out on the basis of logic and for all we know some of these may even be living among us. Nevertheless it seems conceivable that it be argued that (α')

is logically false. In his comprehensive survey, *Recent Work in Epistemic Logic*, W Lenzen mentions in the second chapter that there have been various attempts to explicate the concept of belief in terms of probability notions. Accordingly the statement '*a* believes that *p*' may be analysed to mean that the subjective probability assigned to *p* by *a* is at least equal to $\frac{1}{2}+\varepsilon$ or in symbols: $Pr_a(p) \geqslant \frac{1}{2}+\varepsilon$. It follows then that $Ba \sim p$ iff $Pr_a(\sim p) \geqslant \frac{1}{2}+\varepsilon$. Thus $Pr_a(\sim p) = 1 - Pr_a(p) \geqslant \frac{1}{2}+\varepsilon$, that is $\frac{1}{2}-\varepsilon \geqslant Pr_a(p)$, which means that $\sim Bap$. But then unquestionably $\sim Bap$ is logically incompatible with Bap. Hence $Ba \sim p$ which has just formally been shown to amount to $\sim Bap$ must also be incompatible with Bap!

We might gain greater clarity if we considered the general question whether ϕar is consistent with $\phi a \sim r$? It seems that dyadic predicates may be divided into two groups, one consisting of those which may be regarded genuinely dyadic and the other which are only spuriously so. It appears that there is no inconsistency in asserting both ϕar and $\phi a \sim r$ in the case of the former but there is in the case of the latter.

For example let $\phi_1 ar$ be '*a* says at *t* that he weighs more than 120 lb'. This is clearly compatible with $\phi_1 a \sim r$, that is, '*a* says at *t* that it is false that he weighs more than 120 lb'. There is no problem in imagining the same person uttering on the same occasion contradictory sentences. We note that ϕ_1 is a genuine dyadic predicate since it denotes the relation of uttering between a person and a sentence.

Now let $\phi_2 ar$ be '*a* weighs more than 120 lb'. This sentence is clearly not compatible with $\phi_2 ar$. ϕ_2 is not a genuinely dyadic predicate. It may perhaps give the impression of being one, since it could be looked upon as if it predicated the relation of weighing more, between a person and 120 lb. In fact however it is a monadic predicate since the 120 lb is merely an adverbial qualifier helping to determine the kind of weight *a* has. It might thus be suggested that that question whether or not Bap is consistent with $Ba \sim p$ depends how we treated the predicate B; that is, it depends whether we would assign it to the first or to the second group of dyadic predicates.

Now on the assumption that Bap and $Ba \sim p$ are incompatible, we may proceed as follows:

(2b)	$\sim p \rightarrow Ba \sim p$	by substituting $\sim p/p$ in (*P2*)
(2d)	$Ba \sim p \rightarrow \sim Bap$	given that $Ba \sim p$ rules out Bap
(2e)	$\sim p \rightarrow \sim Bap$	(2b) & (2d) & Hypothetical Syllogism
(2f)	$Bap \rightarrow p$.	(2e), Contraposition

Thus we have derived logically (2f) [which is (*P1*)] from (*P2*). Consequently (*P2*) may be viewed as the most basic thesis concerning privileged access, for both (*P1*) and (*P3*) are implied by it.

Now we may look at some further principles that have been suggested. One of these is what Alston has called the Principle of Self-Warrant which states that propositions describing one's own mental states are always warranted or that every belief in such a proposition is a justified belief. In symbols, *(P4) Bap → JBap*. One may easily be tempted to rush to the conclusion that *(P4)* is not an independent thesis and that it plainly follows from *(P2)* plus the meaning of *JB*. After all, one might argue, *JBap* amounts to saying that *a*'s belief in *p* is warranted because on the basis of the relevant knowledge *a* possesses the likelihood of *p* is sufficiently high. But if it is given that *Bap* because of *(P2)* i.e. *Bap → p*, *a* is provided with full guarantee not merely that the likelihood of *p* is sufficiently high but that it is of maximum weight i.e. that *p* is certainly true. Surely then regardless of what degree of likelihood is generally required for a proposition to have for it to be warranted, absolute certainty cannot fail to qualify.

It may therefore come as a surprise to find that this could be denied. Let us recall that in Chapter One we said 'Many philosophers hold that *a* is not justified in believing that *p* even if *p* can be established on the basis of what *a* knows, as long as *a* himself is not aware of the way this is to be done'. Some may go slightly further and insist that *a* is not justified in believing that *p* even though he has established the credibility of *p*, in the case where he is unaware that the method he used to establish the credibility of *p* is sanctioned by the tenets of rationality and perhaps even if he is merely unable to say why it is legitimate. For example, let us suppose that in order to determine whether a given liquid was acid I immerse litmus paper in it and upon observing the paper turning red I pronounce the liquid acid. Some philosophers would maintain that if I actually had no idea that this was a commonly practised method among chemists wanting to determine the presence of acid, nor that it was objectively reasonable to hold that acidity and the reddening of litmus paper go hand in hand on account of the massive inductive evidence available, and if I had no other reason for using litmus paper but that I had a dream last night in which I was assured that this is an effective method—then my confidence in my conclusion remains without justification. We may note in passing that one might go even further and refuse to be satisfied even if I were fully aware that there is overwhelming inductive evidence that the colour of the paper is a sign of the presence of acid, as long as I am unable to offer a good reason why inductive evidence is to count as acceptable evidence for any hypothesis. It might then be insisted that I justify the belief that the 'good reason' I have offered deserves to be regarded as such. Obviously this can't go on forever if there is to be such a thing as justified belief. We shall not pursue here any further the problem of the regress that might arise from the need to justify the justification of the justification and so on.

However, consider what happens if we adopt the view that as a minimum it is required that *a* be aware that his way of justifying a belief is considered rationally a legitimate way. Now it is clearly conceivable that *a* should believe that *p* and at the same time fail to believe that it provides—or even positively believe that it does not provide—on its own, sufficient justification for believing in the existence of the mental state referred to by *p*. Surely, such a position need not be condemned as incoherent. After all recently a number of reputable philosophers have denied some or all the doctrines of privileged access, and if it is thought to make sense to maintain that *Bap* & $\sim p$ is possibly true then it is very hard to insist that it is wrong to go somewhat further and suggest that not only sometimes but in fact half of the time *a* is mistaken about his own mental states. Granting all this implies that, where *a* believes that it is the concensus among philosophers that *Bap* does not render *p* likely to the degree required for a belief in *p* to become warranted, then it is clearly possible to have *Bap* & $\sim JBap$ in contradistinction to (**P4**).

Another principle that suggests itself is (**P5**) *JBap* → *Bap*. It seems to me that if the earlier principles are granted, then (**P5**) follows automatically. The reason is that we cannot establish the credibility of the belief that *p* unless *a* believes that *p*, in other words *JBap* can only be true when *Bap* is true which amounts to affirming the validity of (**P5**). For a moment it might seem that it is possible to question this; after all from (**P4**) *JBap*, we may infer only that *Bap* is sufficient to guarantee the truth of *JBap*, but not that it is also necessary. It appears to be compatible with all the doctrines of privileged access that there should also exist some other, objective method (e.g. the application of a brainscanning machine) so that *Tap* → *JBap* where *Tap* means 'a test conducted by a reliable apparatus indicates to *a* that *p*', in which case *JBap* need not presuppose *Bap*.

This argument has however only shown that (**P4**) on its own does not imply (**P5**). But suppose we ask : regardless whether *Tap* is or is not true, is it the case that *Bap* or that *Ba*$\sim p$? Recall that it follows from (**P3**) ($\sim Wap$), that one or the other must be true. Suppose that *Ba*$\sim p$ is true then it follows from its conjunction with (**P1**), that $\sim p$. But if it is known with certainty that $\sim p$ is true then no machine, regardless how reliable in the past, can confer rationality on a belief in *p*. So we cannot have *JBap* unless *Bap* is the case; thus *JBap* → *Bap*. We may conclude our list by advancing (**P6**) *p* → *JBap* and (**P7**) *JBap* → *p*, which are obviously derivable from earlier principles. (**P6**) clearly follows from (**P2**) and (**P4**) by Hypothetical Syllogism and (**P7**) follows from (**P5**) and (**P1**) also by Hypothetical Syllogism.

To summarise : in this section we have thus investigated the various logical relations that might exist among the different statements concerning privileged access. Probably the most interesting we have discovered has been that if certain simple presuppositions are granted then in reality there is but a single principle governing *p*-like statements from which all the others may be shown to follow logically. That single principle is (*P2*). As we saw, (*P2*) entails (*P3*) provided we assume that for every *p* if *p* is a mental statement so is ∼ *p*. If we are also permitted to assume that necessarily no person can hold simultaneously contradictory beliefs then (*P1*) follows as well. Then again (*P5*) has been shown to follow directly from (*P3*). We have also seen that on a sufficiently lenient view with regard to what amounts to justified belief, (*P4*) may also be inferred. And the last two principles (*P6*) and (*P7*) can be shown to follow without any extra presuppositions.

I believe that these results provide a good illustration of the usefulness of elementary epistemic logic. It seems obvious that if we had restricted ourselves to employing in our reasoning informal, ordinary English only, our arguments would have had to be longer, more cumbersome and considerably more difficult to follow.

Section 2

An attempt to refute the thesis of privileged access

Lately a number of philosophers have come to deny the validity of some or all the theorems concerning the special status of propositions making assertions about one's current mental states. As indicated in the previous section a discussion of their arguments would not serve our purposes since it would not provide much scope for the use of formal epistemic logic. However, I shall consider one very recent argument that provides a stunning illustration of the potency of this important tool of reasoning. It concerns a remarkably ambitious paper by J J MacIntosh in which he claims to have proven the falsity of a considerable number of basic doctrines concerning privileged access—among them Alston's theses of infallibility, omniscience and self-warrant.[4] I shall limit my discussion to a few lines where he advances a proof of a preliminary theorem concerning the veracity of sets of beliefs a person may have.

I propose to show that MacIntosh has committed at least one error, which effectively deprives all his claims of any defensible support. I shall, however, also attempt to make a constructive point. All men are liable to error. Intelligence is not to make no mistakes but to utilise some readily available methods of detecting these inevitable lapses. I shall outline some of the symptoms that may help us to diagnose the infirmities of our reasoning processes in some cases.

On page 147 we are presented with a proof 'that if anyone, say *a*, believes that s/he has a false belief, then they *do* have a false belief'. That is, if we take Bp: a believes that p, Fp: Bp & $\sim p$, and s for $(\exists p)Fp$ then inevitably $Bs \rightarrow s$. It is a very compact reduction proof:

(1) Bs Assumption
(2) $\sim s$ Assumption
(3) Bs & $\sim s$ (1) & (2) Conj.
(4) Fs (3) defn. of F
(5) $(\exists p)Fp$ (4) E.G. But this contradicts (2)! Hence:
(6) $(\exists p)Fp$ i.e. s Q.E.D.

Now of course $(\exists p)Fp$ is equivalent to $(\exists p)(Fp$ & $(p = s))$ v $(\exists p)(Fp$ & $(p \neq s))$, in which—as MacIntosh believes he has just shown—the left disjunct is inconsistent, and therefore we have (7) $(\exists p)Fp$ & $(p \neq s)$, that is:

> if you believe you have a false belief then you do have, and the belief is not the belief that you have a false belief.

Without going into any further details I shall merely mention that after an additional seven steps MacIntosh arrives at the following triad:

$$(\exists p)Fp \ \& \ \sim B(\exists p)Fp \ \& \ BB(\exists p)Fp$$

which he claims shows decisively that at least some of the doctrines concerning privileged access must be false. Indeed $(\exists p)Fp$ & $\sim B(\exists p)Fp$ which is s & $\sim Bs$ contradicts $s \rightarrow Bs$, that is, it contradicts (*P1*) the so-called Principle of Infallibility.

It is superfluous to examine some of the debatable presuppositions that were employed in the foregoing argument since it will become entirely obvious that there exist no plausible set of premises which could help MacIntosh's enterprise get off the ground. Let me begin by stating that it seems no exaggeration to claim that should MacIntosh's conclusion (7) gain wide acceptance, a whole intellectual revolution would follow, demanding the acquisition of radically different habits of thought about the nature of reality. Let us imagine, for instance, a not entertaining any doubts concerning his beliefs at any time before t. MacIntosh would allow that each of a's beliefs could be true. At t, however, a develops a belief represented by s. Are we now forced to postulate that at t some event of the past that has actually taken place is somehow cancelled retroactively, so as to permit one of a's true beliefs to turn false? No, it seems preferable to postulate that from the beginning one of a's beliefs had to be false; also perhaps because of the ever present possibility that a person may eventually develop a belief in s (regardless of the nature of the beliefs he happens to hold but as a result of a peculiar state of mind brought on by external events or by intoxication, drugs etc.) nobody ever starts with a set of completely true beliefs.

But then does not something more menacing also follow, namely, that irrespective of their number, *all* my beliefs at all times must be false? For suppose I have n beliefs, then one of these, say p_1, is false. Suppose that as time goes by I forget p_1 and believe only in $n-1$ propositions. It will have to be conceded that among these too there is bound to be at least one false belief, e.g., p_2. But then I forget p_2 and so on. Thus from the beginning all of p_1, p_2 must be false. One of the mindboggling implications that follows is that regardless of what p may stand for, if I believe that p, then no one in the world would believe that $\sim p$, since that would make both p and its denial false. To avoid such consequences we might be driven into postulating that like a bad penny which one never loses, the memory of false beliefs is retained forever.

We need however not be concerned with any of this, nor about the indefinitely many more equally disconcerting implications that could be shown also to follow from s, since it may safely be asserted that the probability of its being true is not above zero. To spot the simple error in the previous formal argument, all we need is to ask, what precisely is the set of individuals over which the variable p occurring in $(\exists p)Fp$ ranges? In particular, we want to know, does the domain contain s itself? If it does, then we may say that we are dealing here with

$$(s^+)(\sim p_1 \lor \sim p_2 \lor \cdots \lor \sim p_n \lor \sim s)$$

where $p_1, p_2, \ldots, p_n$ are all of a's other beliefs. If it does not, then we have

$$(s^-)(\sim p_1 \lor \sim p_2 \lor \cdots \lor \sim p_n).$$

We note that the assertion that (s^+) is true amounts to saying that (s^-) (the last disjunct of the right hand side of the first expression) is false. That is, to assert s^+ is to deny the possibility that it is the last disjunct of the right hand side of that expression which is true; thus it is to affirm that only the remaining propositions are candidates for being true, i.e. only the propositions that appear in (s^-). Clearly then, there are no two possibilities; s definitely makes no reference to itself; s is outside the domain of p. But then obviously Step (5) of MacIntosh's derivation is illegitimate as we cannot existentially generalise from Fs to $(\exists p)Fp$ since s is the one of a's beliefs that is outside our universe of discourse!

It is possible of course to substitute a legitimate expression (1*), for (1) such that s is included in the set of propositions of which a believes that it contains a false member, i.e.

$$(1^*) \quad B[(\exists p)Fp \lor \sim(\exists p)Fp].$$

(1*) is an innocuous expression with which all who are aware of the Law of Excluded Middle will agree, and nothing interesting can be derived with its aid.

As mentioned earlier, errors are unavoidable. However, under certain circumstances fairly reliable methods are available through which one may establish that a mistake in reasoning must have been committed somewhere. Once a person is aware of this much and the area of search is not unmanageably large, he is bound to identify the error.

In the context of our example, the emergence of such hair-raising consequences—e.g. that either all our beliefs are false or we are incapable of forgetting a false belief—should alert one that something must be wrong with the reasoning that led to them.

Suppose, however, that one has never had the chance of recoiling from the implications of *s* simply because one has never thought of examining the implications of *s*. It should make no difference. I submit that being confronted by *s* alone should be quite sufficient to convince one that no correct chain of reasoning could have led to it. After all, *s* is clearly asserting a claim that is almost sure to be empirically false and at any rate is certainly not logically true. As indicated earlier, no tight causal connection exists between the contents of a given set of propositions and *a*'s propensity to believe any of them. Sometimes *a* believes a falsehood because he has been presented with very convincing evidence or because of strong wishful thinking or because he has been injected with a large dose of the gullibility serum. In any case it is logically possible that extraneous factors could determine what a person believes. How is it then conceivable that a sound formal proof be given that if *a* has this or that belief then of necessity some other proposition must be false?

But a somewhat deeper point seems to be involved here. Even if *s* on its own were an entirely innocuous statement, then merely the alleged fact that it leads directly to the denial of a variety of a propositions concerning privileged access should arouse strong suspicion about the validity of its derivation. When it comes to such momentous and ultimate questions like whether we have free will or whether the future is real, one never arrives at a decisive answer through a concise, neat and purely logical method of reasoning. At most what happens is that the advocate of, say, the thesis that the future is unreal succeeds in deriving his conclusion with the help of several assumptions that, because they look inoffensive, seem more acceptable than the assumptions hitherto believed to be necessary for maintaining the unreality of the future. In our case MacIntosh set out to show that I may for instance believe myself to be in pain when as a matter of objective fact I am not. But this is contrary to the deeply entrenched, cherished beliefs of many, concerning the special status of mental statements. Surely, faced with such a deep issue, MacIntosh cannot realistically expect to accomplish his aim through a few swift, purely logical strokes without recourse to some hypothesis that is not necessarily true.

Now of course many will claim that the problem as to whether avowals of inner experiences form a special category in themselves does not lie at as deep a level as these other problems. The issue of privileged access is not really a profound conceptual issue but one that might be resolved by such practical means as more careful introspection by specially trained subjects; more sophisticated methods of psychoanalysis, or some future brain-scanning device. Should this really be the correct view, then my point should apply with even greater force. If indeed what we are confronted with here is an empirical question, then there is certainly no chance that pure epistemic logic unaided by any factual premises will yield some useful result.

In conclusion, I trust that it is not misleading to claim that the extraordinary argument to refute the various theses of privileged access dramatically illustrates the vitality of elementary formal epistemic logic. It is a common characteristic of highly powerful tools that when misused the results may be devastating. The fact that it is possible for a competent practitioner of formal reasoning to go so spectacularly astray through the use of rudimentary epistemic logic is, I believe, a true mark of the potency of this branch of applied logic.

3

Fallibilism and Possibilities

Section 1

Practical and metaphysical theses about knowledge claims

One of the best uses of elementary epistemic logic is as an aid in defining the central notions of epistemic logic. A definition, as Milton has put it is that which refines the pure essence of things from the circumstance, and therefore an economically and rigorously formulated explicative definition can be regarded as the paradigm device for providing maximum elucidation of a concept. For effective accomplishment of this task philosophers have as a rule turned to the formalism of epistemic logic rather than looking to ordinary language (which they expected to yield much more cumbersome, vague and less transparent results). In this and the next chapter we shall discuss attempts to define formally some of the major concepts in epistemology concerning the scope and limits of knowledge and the status of cognitive statements in general. The main objective in this chapter will be to find an adequate definition of 'fallibilism' and 'epistemic possibility'. In the next chapter we shall try to define 'scepticism'.

The majority of thinkers agree that one of the important lessons of history is that in science there are no absolute guarantees. No matter how well founded a given belief may be, its truth cannot be established with ultimate certainty. A hypothesis *h* may be highly credible, even to the extent that it is perfectly rational to act upon it as well as to claim that we know it, and yet we are never justified in having entirely unreserved confidence in *h*. We may hold many hypotheses that represent genuine knowledge of nature, yet no hypothesis of ours is fully immune from future revision; they are all corrigible.

The thesis of the ever-present possibility of error is called *fallibilism*. It is often assumed that the difference between the cognate doctrines of fallibilism and scepticism lies essentially in the degree of limitation they ascribe to the inquiring human mind. A sceptic with respect to a species of propositions denies that we can ever *know* any member of that species, while the fallibilist may concede knowledge but not certainty. I believe, therefore, that in this preliminary section it is important to emphasise that there exists another fundamental difference as well. Fallibilism—unlike many forms of scepticism—is to most people who subscribe to it a 'practical', as distinct from a mere 'metaphysical', thesis. Working scientists are unlikely to engage in lengthy discussions of the problem of how we know of the existence of an external world or of the problem of induction yet they are keenly interested in the idea of the change in fortune that may befall even the best of hypotheses. The reader may be reminded of Hume's famous admission that his scepticism concerning the validity of induction, while very serious, is nevertheless something he puts out of his mind once he leaves his study. It should be different with fallibilism; and awareness of a certain degree of tenuousness attaching to all knowledge claims should be with us at all times.

One famous contemporary physicist, K G Denbigh, has recently provided some fascinating concrete examples illustrating a ubiquitous practical principle which alone should prevent us from being capable of securing any hypothesis. The principle asserts the invalidity of an inductive argument based on a biased sample class. No matter how many members of the sample class, which is the class of observed individuals that have P, turned out also to have had Q, we cannot generalise that all P's are Q's in case each one of these individuals also had F. It is possible after all that not all P's are Q's: particulars having P but no F may not have Q either. The principle is, of course, of fairly common knowledge. What is so remarkable is that, in many cases, for centuries no common 'F' to invalidate a given generalisation is discerned by anyone until some entirely unsuspected feature forces itself on the attention of scientists.

One of Denbigh's noteworthy examples in his excellent book involves predictions made not so long ago concerning what the temperature of the sun is going to be in a couple of years.[1] The calculations were made on the basis of judicious assessment of the relevant constants with the aid of the cooling law of hot substances. However, the predicted results were nowhere near the actual results. The reason, as is well known, was that a crucial tacit assumption was made, an assumption regarded as not even meriting a second thought since its denial would have been thought of as the height of absurdity. The assumption was that the sun is not gaining heat by some internal non-chemical process. There were not many laws of physics at that time that had received more overwhelming confirmation than the law of the conservation of energy and the law of immutability of substances. Nothing would have sounded much more preposterous a hundred years ago than that heat is being generated inside the sun by the conversion of hydrogen into helium.

Nevertheless, our assumptions concerning heat-generating processes which seemed so irrevocably well-founded, turned out to have been based on a sample class—though vast in size—that was biased in an unexpected manner. All the members of the sample class that had obeyed the widely known laws of cooling had the bias of sharing a certain significant feature, the feature of being associated with relatively low temperature and pressure. There was therefore no real basis for assuming that the case of the sun would be subject to laws essentially similar to those governing the members of the sample class. We had never before experimented with temperature and pressure even approximately as high as inside the sun. Under extraordinary circumstances it is plausible to entertain a hitherto unheard-of process of heat generation.

Thus one of the reasons it is appropriate for a scientist to be a fallibilist is that even the most firmly rooted generalisation may not hold universally and might be seen to break down under entirely novel circumstances.

In this chapter I propose to offer as precise a statement of fallibilism as I can. Lately there have been a number of attempts to provide a rigorous, formal definition of fallibilism, none of which seems to have been successful. The failure, I believe, is really due to the entirely unexpected nature of the task. The thesis which I seem to have rendered adequately enough in plain English may look transparently clear and therefore one may well be expected to go straight ahead and quickly formulate a simple expression of it. Thus it takes some time before one realises the existence of so many unsuspected difficulties. I believe it is philosophically very instructive to see some of the hidden traps along the way to a satisfactory formulation.

Section 2

The indefinite scope for error

In an informative paper that touches upon a number of basic aspects of epistemology, L S Carrier expresses his support for cognitivism (i.e. opposition for scepticism) about any group of propositions and argues in favour of what looks like fallibilism with respect to all empirical propositions. Like Denbigh, Carrier also presents an all-pervasive practical obstacle, which in his view stands in the way of achieving certainty. Carrier contends that in the process of trying to establish any empirical proposition there is always scope for indefinitely many errors. He declares that it 'would require too much of finite creatures to expect them to be in a position to know an indefinitely long conjunction of propositions each asserting that a particular error has been committed'. Carrier lays down the principle:

(2) $\sim Ka \sim Mae$, i.e. an individual a does not know that he is not
mistaken that e (where e stands for an empirical statement).

The following is the essence of his explanation:[2]

> Empirical propositions are not only inherently open to falsification, but they also
> leave room for completely undetected error. One can still know empirical facts if
> we grant premise (2), but to have knowledge that there is no mistaking these facts
> would have to be denied, for this would require too much of finite creatures. The
> last point can be put logically in this way: a's being mistaken that e amounts to an
> indefinitely long disjunction, each of whose disjuncts states a way in which a
> would be mistaken, i.e. $Mae \rightarrow p \lor q \lor r \cdots \lor n$. So a's *not* being mistaken that e
> is logically equivalent to an indefinitely long *conjunction* each of whose conjuncts
> states a denial of a particular way in which a would be mistaken (i.e. Ka
> $\sim Mae \leftrightarrow Ka \sim p \& Ka \sim q \& Ka \sim r \& \cdots Ka \sim n$). But surely a does not know all
> these things.

Thus Carrier would approve of

$$(\phi_1) \quad (\exists e)Kae \& (e) \sim Ka \sim Mae$$

as a rigorous, formal expression of fallibilism as well as cognitivism.

All this sounds reasonable, and thus it comes somewhat as a surprise to
find that (ϕ_1) is involved in an irreparably damaging error.

Let e_1 stand for a particular empirical statement and 'B' for 'believes
that', then, suppose that Kae_1:

$Ka(e_1 \lor \sim Bae_1)$	By the Law of Addition
$Ka \sim (\sim e_1 \& Bae)$	By De Morgan
$Ka \sim Mae_1$	By Defn. of M

Thus for any e, if a knows that e, then it follows also that a knows also that
he is not mistaken that e (as long as a knows the Law of Addition and De
Morgan's Law). Thus (ϕ_1) is inconsistent. It follows that Carrier's (2) is not
merely an expression of fallibilism. The denial of $Ka \sim Mae$ entails the
denial of Kae. Thus (2) is an expression of scepticism, something Carrier
decidedly wanted to avoid.

Some philosophers may not be entirely happy with this proof, wondering
whether Kae may be said to imply logically $Ka(e_1 \lor \sim Bae_1)$, that is,
whether we are permitted to add to e_1 just any proposition regardless how
irrelevant. We can avoid this problem by showing (ϕ_1) to be inconsistent in
a different way, which is almost as concise as the first way:

$Kae_1 \rightarrow Ka \sim (\sim e_1)$	By the Law of Double Negation

$Ka \sim (\sim e_1 \ \& \ Bae_1)$ — Since if a knows that one of the conjuncts of a conjunction is false, he knows that the conjunction is false

$Ka \sim Mae_1$ — By Defn. of M

Section 3

The logical possibility of all beliefs

Recently Susan Haack has written an interesting paper exploring the possibility of formalising the thesis of fallibility.[3] After rejecting a number of preliminary attempts she advances

$$(F_4) \quad (p) \Diamond Bp$$

as a plausible candidate for properly expressing the universal fallibility of the human mind. (F_4) seems to affirm that we are capable of believing any proposition irrespective of whether it is true or false, and thus any one of our beliefs may be false.

Haack then points out that if (F_4) were indeed an adequate representation of fallibilism then its denial

$$(D) \quad (\exists p) \sim \Diamond B \sim p$$

would amount to what may be called *dogmatism*. Expression (D) is, however, not strong enough since it does not imply that we actually have any true beliefs. Thus dogmatism is more adequately represented by

$$(D^*) \quad (\exists p) [\Box(Bp \supset p) \ \& \ \sim \Diamond B \sim p].$$

Consequently fallibilism is represented by

$$(F^*) \quad (p) [\sim \Box(Bp \supset p) \lor \Diamond B \sim p]$$

First, let me point out that there seems to be a simple formal error here : how could Haack attempt to replace (F_4) by (F^*) when the two are logically equivalent? It is easily seen that they are. Clearly $(F_4) \rightarrow (F^*)$ by substituting $\sim p$ for p and using the Law of Addition. Now, the first disjunct of (F^*), $\sim \Box(Bp \supset p)$, is logically equivalent to $\Diamond(Bp \ \& \ \sim p)$ (from the definition of '$\Box$' and '$\supset$'). Hence (F^*) logically implies $(p) [(\Diamond Bp \ \& \ \Diamond \sim p) \lor \Diamond B \sim p]$, which entails $(p) [\Diamond Bp \lor \Diamond B \sim p]$, since $((a \ \& \ b) \lor c) \rightarrow (a \lor c)$ and this entails (F_4), i.e. $(p) \Diamond Bp$.[4] We have thus shown the logical equivalence of (F^*) and (F_4).

This, however, is a relatively minor point. The far more serious difficulty is that Haack seems to have conflated two radically different kinds of possibilities. She employs the symbol '$\diamond$' and it is evident that she assigns to it its normal sense, namely, 'logically possible' which is far from being sufficient for the purpose at hand. $\diamond Bp$ means no more than 'it is not self-contradictory to assert that Bp'. This of course is compatible with saying that in fact it is *never* the case that Bp and even with saying that there is an *immutable law of nature* making it impossible for Bp to be the case. Thus the expression (F_4) has nothing to do with fallibilism. For suppose there was an immutable law of nature that for some p, whenever Bp then inevitably p was true. In other words we suppose now that it is nomically impossible for anyone to believe certain false propositions, then

(i) $(p)\diamond Bp$ may remain true, since it does not amount to a *contradiction* to assert Bp for any p, even if false;
(ii) fallibilism would, of course, be false.

It follows therefore, that (F_4) is compatible with the falsity of fallibilism. It should be added that (F_4) is so useless that it is not only compatible with the mere denial of total fallibilism but also with the doctrine that we are all absolutely infallible or even perfectly omniscient; that is we hold only true beliefs and do not fail to believe anything that is true! This follows at once from the fact that even if it was never nomically possible for anyone to hold any false proposition, this would not render Bp self-contradictory and thus $\diamond Bp$ could hold for every p in spite of the immutable law of nature preventing anyone of us from holding a false belief.

It should be noted that this kind of oversight is not specifically associated with efforts to formalise the notion of fallibilism. For example Richard Feldman has recently offered the following informal definition:

(F_1) It is possible for S to know that p even if S does not have logically conclusive evidence to justify believing that p.

and he goes on to explain:[5]

What it amounts to is the claim that people can know things on the basis of nondeductive arguments. That is, they can know things on the basis of inductive, perceptual, or testimonial evidence that does not entail what it is evidence for.

It is not difficult to see that Feldman's (F_1) fails once more for the reason that it is compatible with perfect infallibilism. Suppose E is some superior 'inductive, perceptual or testimonial evidence'. Then all that Feldman tells us is that it is not the case that E is logically conclusive or that E entails p. In other words (F_1) merely denies that $\Box(Ep \supset p)$. This of course permits $Ep \supset p$ to be true. But the latter is sufficient to guarantee that not one proposition we have established by approved empirical methods will *in fact* ever turn out to be false.

Similarly David Stove in his *Popper and After*—a remarkably witty and at the same time vitally important book—says, in reference to fallibilism:[6]

> ...it asserts no more than the *logical possibility* of the conjunction of the evidence for any given scientific theory, with the negation of that theory.

It is quite obvious, however, that if fallibilism is to be a doctrine which ascribes a practically significant imperfection to all our knowledge claims, it must assert more than the mere logical possibility that our theories are false. To be more explicit: it must ascribe *epistemic possibility*. Of course simply to state this would not accomplish our goal since the notion of 'epistemic possibility' is not clearer than the notion of 'fallibilism'. In the last section of this chapter we shall see that as soon as a definition of 'fallibilism' is found, a definition of epistemic possibility automatically follows.

Section 4

No infallible methods

Peter L Mott has published a paper discussing Haack's suggestion.[7] In a somewhat roundabout and lengthy way he shows that (F^*) logically implies (F_4) which he declares to be absurd. Mott claims:

> ...if you believe that 1 is a number then you cannot believe that 1 is the first letter of the alphabet.

Mott's point does not seem to be correct. A statement of the form p & $\sim p$ is logically false, however, $B(p$ & $\sim p)$ is not a contradiction and logic does not tell us that it must be false. Mott's example concerning the number 1 may be absurd because it is not possible *psychologically* for anyone to believe it. That, however, does not imply that $\Diamond Bp$ is false for any p, since that merely claims that Bp is not *logically* impossible.

However, Mott could have raised his objection by using a different sentence. For example let p be 's has a toothache', and assume that p is false. In this case there are philosophers who would insist that $\sim \Diamond Bsp$ since the very notion of pain analytically implies that it is the sort of thing that s cannot have without s sincerely believing that she has it and vice versa.

Another possibility might be to take p as 'q & $\sim Bsq$', in which case we are once more committed to $\sim \Diamond Bsp$ since otherwise we would have to claim

$\Diamond(Bsq\ \&\ Bs \sim Bsq)$. The bracketed expression would be ruled by some to be necessarily false since it necessarily follows from Bsq that $BsBsq$.

Even so, we still should not conclude that Haack's formalisation is faulty, since fallibilism is generally assumed to be a somewhat restricted doctrine. Those who maintain the incorrigibility of avowals of inner experiences would exempt such avowals from being included in the doctrine. Haack herself said so explicitly elsewhere :[8]

> However, epistomologists have often thought that, with respect to certain *kinds* of belief—belief about one's own immediate sense-experience are a favoured example—people may be infallible: they are liable to have false beliefs about astronomy, geography . . . etc., but they are not liable to be mistaken about whether they are in pain, seeing a red patch . . . etc.

Consequently, provided there were no other objections, these epistemologists could avail themselves of $(e)\Diamond Be$ as an adequate expression of fallibilism by adding that e ranges over empirical propositions.

Be that as it may, Mott proceeds to advance his own suggestion for the formalisation of fallibilism. He proposes that the doctrine is best defined as the claim that there are no infallible methods of securing knowledge. To be more precise, it is the claim that there exists no procedure δ such that

(a)   applying δ always leads to a correct decision whether p and
(b) S's decisions are always correctly determined by the experimenter.

To express this in symbols, fallibilism amounts to the denial of the conjunction :

(D_1) $(p)(\delta p \supset p)$

(D_2) $(p) \sim \Diamond (B\delta p\ \&\ \sim \delta p)$

where 'δ' is called by Mott a Cartesian functor.

There are, however, a great number of objections to Mott's suggestion, and I do not know how he would react to them :

(1) Let us suppose that 'δ' denotes any method whatever, then as long as δ has never been applied to test the veracity of *any* p, $(p) \sim \delta p$ is true, and this logically implies the truth of (D_1) $(p)(\delta p \supset p)$. Thus we are driven to the absurd conclusion that we are entitled to proclaim the doctrine of perfect infallibilism as long as there is *some* method that has never been applied to *any* p. This in fact amounts to the conclusion that we are infallible under all practical circumstances!

It does not seem possible to salvage the core of (D_1) by replacing it by

$$(D_1')\quad (\exists p)\delta p\ \&\ (p)(\delta p \supset p)$$

which is incompatible with δ being a method that has never been applied. (D_1') is not a useful expression since, for example, if δ has been applied to no more than a single p, which happens to be true and yielded positive results, (D_1') would be satisfied.

On the other hand, to suggest that we should have

$$(D_1'') \quad (p)\delta p \,\&\, (\delta p \supset p)$$

seems to have the obvious defect of claiming that we *actually* know everything there is to be known, which of course even those who hold the doctrine of perfect infallibility concede to be false. They might *perhaps* maintain that omniscience is a possibility but this cannot be expressed as

$$(D_1''') \quad \Diamond(p)\delta p \,\&\, (\delta p \supset p)$$

since this merely asserts logical possibility of omniscience without indicating that it is practically within reach.

(2) Let us ignore what we have said so far and assume that $D_1 \,\&\, D_2$ adequately defines dogmatic epistemology. If so then $(\exists p) \sim (\delta p \supset p)$ would have to express fallibilism. But surely it is not a sufficiently strong expression since $(\exists p) \sim (\delta p \supset p)$ would be true as soon as there was one specific proposition p_1 whose truth has not been successfully established. Fallibilism says, however, much more: that with respect to *all* propositions of a certain kind there must be some reservation.

Incidentally, it may be noted that Mott seems not merely to have failed to capture in the language of symbolic logic the idea of fallibilism but there is also a subtle error in the way he renders it informally. He writes:

Let us characterise fallibilism as the doctrine that *there are no Cartesian functors.*

Fallibilism says much more than that. The fallibilist wishes not merely to deny the existence of a secure method which '*always* leads to a correct decision whether p' but even just that of the existence of a secure enough method leading to absolute certainty with respect to *even one* empirical proposition.

Oddly enough, $(\exists p) \sim (\delta p \supset p)$, besides being too weak to express the full scope of fallibilism, also seems too strong! Fallibilism implies only that there is no absolute certainty about any of our beliefs, but does not go as far as to claim that all, many or even that some of our beliefs are decidedly false. $(\exists p) \sim (\delta p \supset p)$ is, however, equivalent to $(\exists p)(\delta p \,\&\, \sim p)$, asserting that we do hold at least one false belief.

(3) An examination of (D_2) may give rise to even stronger objections. If (D_2) were adequate then its denial would have to be supposed to yield

fallibilism. But the denial of (D_2) amounts to

$$(\bar{D}_2) \quad \sim(p) \sim \Diamond(B\delta p \ \& \ \sim \delta) \qquad \text{i.e.} \ (\bar{D}_2) \quad (\exists p)\Diamond(B\delta p) \ \& \ \sim \delta p)$$

which is compatible with δ being a perfectly fool-proof method for establishing the truth of any proposition it is applied to. $(\bar{D}_2)$ says no more than that $B\delta p \ \& \ \sim \delta p$ is logically possible i.e. that there is no logical contradiction in asserting $B\delta p \ \& \ \sim \delta p$. Fallibilism says, of course, more: it says that it is not contrary to any *causal law* to have both $B\delta P$ and $\sim \delta p$; that they are *nomically* co-possible.

Section 5

Nomic implication

Matters could be set right by introducing nomic concepts and by asserting that fallibilism is adequately represented by

$$(D_3) \quad (e)\sim(JBe \ni e)$$

with JB for 'it is justifiably believed that' and '$\ni$' meaning 'if . . . then it follows by law of nature that' or 'if . . . then it is causally necessary that'. (D_3) asserts that for no proposition does the fact that it is justifiably believed, because it is supported by any amount of evidence, constitute a nomic guarantee for its truth.

The obvious objection that will be levelled against (D_3) is that it fails to accomplish what philosophers have set out to accomplish, namely to formulate a definition out of simple logical terms, which $\ni$ is not. In fact, the precise explication of the notion of nomic or causal necessity has been the subject of considerable controversy. It would be inappropriate to attempt defining the relatively transparent notion of fallibilism in terms of the more opaque concept of causal necessity.

Some might think of suggesting

$$(D_4) \quad (e)(Pr(e) < 1)$$

as an expression of fallibilism. (D_4) implies that no amount of justification will allow the value of the probability of an empirical proposition to reach one. (D_4) is undeniably equivalent to fallibilism since $Pr(e) = 1$ amounts precisely to saying that 'e is certain to be true', and fallibilism is a denial of just that. It is important to realise, however, that (D_4) is no use as a philosophical explication. One may, for example, define 'a knows that p' by 'a is cognisant of p', which may be fine in a dictionary, the function of which is to translate a word into other words. Such a translation is not, however, what epistemologists have been looking for. Philosophical value attaches only to a definition in terms of different concepts from those employed in the *definiendum*.

It might still be thought that one could make use of the basic features of probability in our definition of fallibilism without making any reference to probability, but only to elementary epistemic notions. Given that for any proposition e_1 no matter how well grounded our belief in it may be, still the probability of e_1 is less than one, then obviously if e_1 and e_2 are logically independent then $Pr(e_1 \& e_2) < Pr(e_1)$ and of course $Pr(e_1 \& e_2 \& e_3)$ $< Pr(e_1 \& e_2)$ and so on. The suggestion could be made that fallibilism be expressed by

$$(D_5) \quad JBe_1 \& JBe_2 \& \ldots \& JBe_n \& \sim JB(e_1 \& e_2 \ldots e_n)$$

when n is a large enough number.

There is no question about it, (D_5) *is* true. It is, however, not an adequate representation of fallibilism; it is too weak for that. Even if fallibilism were false (D_5) would be true: it may justifiably be believed of each lottery ticket that it will fail to win but not that all of them will fail to win. This, however, is not due to any imperfection in our methods of inquiry. It is due to the fact that it is clearly given that one ticket is definitely going to win as well as that there are many tickets. Thus the probability of any particular ticket's winning is very small.

This suggests that the appropriate way to express fallibilism should be:

$$(D_6) \quad Ke_1 \& Ke_2 \ldots \& Ke_n \& \sim K(e_1 \& e_2 \ldots \& e_n).$$

However, even (D_6) is still too weak. A quick way of showing this is to consider a person s who cares more about one particular proposition e_1, more than about anything else, and spends an inordinate amount of time making sure it is true. The fallibilist should want to say to s that even though he is willing to renounce his knowledge of anything else and has concentrated all his efforts on finding a firm basis for his belief that e_1, he is still not entitled to claim infallibility with respect to it. This of course does not amount to saying that $\sim Kse_1$; such a radical claim would be made by only a sceptic. What the fallibilist says to s is: you may of course know that e_1, but not with absolute certainty. Expression (D_5), which affirms a large number of knowledge claims which s does not make, does not seem to speak to his situation.

Section 6

Degrees of justification

The justification of beliefs admits of degrees. The degree to which a belief needs to be justified in order to be rationally held is not so high as to ensure the truth of that belief. Let us use $JFae$ to mean 'a is justified in having *full* conviction that e' and let us stipulate that $(\alpha)\,(e)(JFae \supset e)$.[9] It then seems reasonable to maintain that fallibilism is adequately expressed by

$$(\phi) \quad (e) \sim JFae.$$

Expression (ϕ) is compatible with there being any number of propositions that may be regarded as highly credible to the extent that it is perfectly rational to act upon them. We are nevertheless not justified in having entirely unreserved confidence in any of them.

Clearly, however, (α) does not amount to a complete definition. It might therefore be suggested that we employ a different notion, one that various philosophers have denoted by C, signifying 'convinced that'. C too represents a stronger belief than B and it has the supposedly great advantage over F that it may fully be defined in terms of already existing notions. W Lenzen in his very helpful survey of epistemic logic argues that C is not a new predicate since it may be shown that

$$(58) \quad Cap \equiv\, \sim Ka \sim Kap.\text{[10]}$$

Hence it might be thought feasible to express fallibilism as

$$(\phi') \quad (e) \sim JCae.$$

Unfortunately, this does not work. After all, the notion of 'justification' yields:

$$\sim JCae \equiv Ra \to\, \sim Cae$$

asserting that 'a is not justified in holding e with conviction' is equivalent to saying 'if a is rational then a is not going to hold e with conviction'. Consequently we may rewrite

$$(\phi') \quad (e)(Ra \to\, \sim Cae), \quad \text{which of course is}$$

$$(e)(Ra \to Ka \sim Kae)$$

by Lenzen's (58). (ϕ') is however unacceptable since it is more destructive than fallibilism. Fallibilism does not deny that we know something whereas, of course, $Ka \sim Kae$ entails $\sim Kae$.

Incidentally, judicious as Lenzen is in general, here he seems to have committed a mistake. Earlier in his book he implies that Cap (as distinct from Bap) is not required for knowledge. But, as we see, his (58) implies otherwise.

Thus we shall make use of the operator F which, even if it may not be fully defined, can be clarified by making several statements about it. First we may assert

$$(p)(JFp \rightarrow JBp) \ \& \ \sim(p)(JBp \rightarrow JFp)$$

where 'p' stands for all sorts of propositions including those which are exempt from coming under the doctrine of fallibilism.

Since there are indefinitely many degrees of justification we may insert between 'JB' and 'JF' the operator 'JC' of which it may be said:

$$(p)(JFp \rightarrow JCp) \ \& \ \sim(p)(JCp \rightarrow JFp) \quad \text{as well as}$$

$$(p)(JCp \rightarrow JBp) \ \& \ \sim(p)(JBp \rightarrow JCp)$$

and we can do the same for any further number of operators representing different degrees of justified belief.

Each valid expression involving these operators contributes to their explication. And there are more such expressions. It may, for example, be asserted that

$$(\exists p_1)(\exists p_2)(JCp_1 \ \& \ JCp_2 \ \& \ \sim JC(p_1 \ \& \ p_2))$$

for the reason indicated before, namely, that rational belief to a given degree in each of a number of propositions does not necessarily carry over into rational belief to *the same degree* in the conjunction of those propositions. It may however still carry over into a rational belief of some lower degree. Consequently, it may also be asserted that

$$(\exists p_1)(\exists p_2)(JCp_1 \ \& \ JCp_2 \ \& \ \sim JC(p_1 \ \& \ p_2) \ \& \ JB(p_1 \ \& \ p_2)).$$

But of course 'F' is unique among all the operators since

$$(p_1)(p_2)(JFp_1 \ \& \ JFp_2 \rightarrow JF(p_1 \ \& \ p_2))$$

is true in its case.

Section 7

Epistemic possibility

Now we are in a position to say something useful about the important notion of 'epistemic possibility'. G E Moore, in a famous passage, pointed out that in general there are three major senses of possible:[11]

(1) *Logical.* It's possible that I should have been seeing exactly what I am seeing and yet should have no eyes. I *might* have been seeing what I do and had no eyes. It's possible that every dog that has ever lived should have climbed a tree.

(2) *Causal.* It's possible that I should have been blind by now. I *might* have been blind now. It's possible that I should have travelled 200 miles since an hour ago.

(3) *Epistemic.* It is possible that Hitler is now (12pm Oct. 26) dead. Hitler *may* be dead.

There have been several attempts to elucidate the concept of epistemic possibility. Paul Teller has, for example, written a paper in which he attempts to improve upon a suggestion by Ian Hacking and in which he produces a series of increasingly more elaborate definitions.[12] However, he does not seem to have managed to get even the most basic things right.

One of his earlier formulations, which he believes conveys roughly the idea of epistemic possibility, is:

D2: It is possible that *p* if and only if

    (a)   *p* is not known to be false

nor (b)   are propositions known which could serve as basis, data or evidence on the strength of which we could come to know that *p* is false.

It should be sufficient to consider but one reason why D2 completely misses the point. Let *h* be 'All copper expands when heated' which may be said to be paradigmatic of a solidly established generalisation. Yet a thoughtful scientist like Denbigh will tell us that because of inevitable practical limitations on the available evidence, *h* could possibly turn out to be false in spite of the overwhelming amount of inductive confirmation it has received. We must ask now, which type of possibility, would he have in mind? Surely not (1), logical possibility, since then all he would be conveying to us is that we are not involved in a contradiction in asserting $\sim h$. That, however, is compatible with *h* being absolutely certain and fully immune to all future revision.

But neither could he mean (2), physical possibility, since there is no sufficient basis for that. That is, there is no justification for maintaining that though *h* is as well confirmed as anything could be, nevertheless it is physically possible that it is false. Reasonable scientists do not claim to know that *h* is definitely false. Should *h* happen to be true, then it is in fact an immutable law of nature that no circumstances will ever arise under which copper fails to expand when heated. But in that case it is physically *impossible* that *h* be violated.

Therefore it is inevitable that the term 'possible' in the present context can mean only (3), epistemic possibility. But scientists do believe that *h*, and they are justified in believing that *h*, therefore, should it also be the case that *h* is true, they *know* that *h*. But if *h* is known to be true then, of course, $\sim h$ is known to be false, and yet it is appropriate to regard at present $\sim h$ as epistemically possible.

Now if we substitute $\sim h$ for p in Teller's definition, it immediately conflicts with the obvious fact that $\sim h$ *may* be known to be false and yet is epistemically possible.

One point still remains to be clarified. Some may find it strange that propositions that are epistemically so differently related to us should be ascribed the same states, namely, as being epistemically possible. After all, Moore's example involving the possibility of Hitler being dead, was expressed at a time when there was no firm evidence that he was alive. Are we really using the same notion when on the one hand we are across the channel in England, having no peace-time means of communications, and therefore can definitely not be regarded as *knowing* that Hitler is not dead already, and thus declare 'Hitler is possibly dead', and on the other hand when speaking of the vastly more remote possibility of h being false?

All puzzlement should, however, disappear once we realise that just like everything else in epistemology, possibilities, too come in different degrees. There are stronger and weaker beliefs, convictions, doubts and justifications, and thus there are stronger and weaker epistemic possibilities. Thus, for example, we may define

$$'p \text{ is epistemically possible' as } \sim JB \sim p$$

implying a fairly strong possibility, since when p is possible we definitely do not know that p is false. In addition we may also define epistemic possibility in weaker ways.

It does not come as a surprise to find that fallibilism too admits indefinitely many degrees. Our expression

$$(e) \sim JFae$$

represents the weakest kind of fallibilism. A stronger kind would be given by, for instance,

$$(e) \sim JCae.$$

Obviously, for any degree of justified belief that is stronger than simple belief, there exists a corresponding degree of fallibilism.

4

Scepticism

Section 1

The universal possibility of error

In this chapter we shall look at the relatively simple notion of 'scepticism'. It is interesting to note that even though advocates of scepticism have existed from early antiquity and the debate around it has not ceased ever since, there is still no generally agreed upon, straightforward and accurate formulation of the doctrine of scepticism.

I believe it will be useful to discuss a recent paper by Nicholas Griffin and Merle Harton who have reviewed various suggestions as to how best define in terms of the symbolism of elementary epistemic logic the thesis that none of us knows anything.[1] In the course of their discussion they consider what they call the thesis of the universal possibility of error, that is,

$$(UPE) \quad (p)(a) \Diamond Map$$

which amounts to saying that it is possible that any given person a should be mistaken with respect to every proposition he holds. They conclude however that (UPE) is unsatisfactory. They point out that by definition if a believes mistakenly that p then p must be false, and therefore $\Box(Map \to \sim p)$ and given the axiom $\Box(p \to q) \to (\Diamond p \to \Diamond q)$ it follows from substituting Map for p, $\sim p$ for q and Modus Ponens that

$$\Diamond Map \to \Diamond \sim p.$$

Suppose now that p is a necessary truth, i.e. $\sim \Diamond \sim p$ then by Modus Tollens we get from the previous expression $\sim \Diamond Map$. Somewhat unexpectedly this result is interpreted by the authors as implying that if p is a necessary truth then it resists even the possibility of error. But then one of the most famous sceptics, Descartes, has contended that there is reason to be sceptical about necessary truth as well because of the possibility of deductive error. Griffin and Harton conclude therefore that (*UPE*) is inadequate, since it is incapable of representing the radical position expoused by Descartes.

Since many people have found this argument seductive it should be quite instructive to examine it more closely. The reasoning may appear plausible as $\sim \Diamond Map$ decidedly says that it is not logically possible to believe p mistakenly, and this happens to be a rather strong statement since even if we were given no more than $\sim Map$ which says merely that *in fact* it is not the case that a mistakenly believes that p it would have been sufficient for reaching the conclusion. After all one cannot attribute an erroneous belief to a not only if it is given that that it is logically impossible for a to be in error but even if it is just affirmed that it is decidedly not true that a is in error.

Perhaps the best way to get on to the route leading to a clear view on this matter is to use the approach taken by Griffin and Harton in order to advance a much more sweeping claim, namely, that nobody has ever in the past nor will in the future be mistaken with respect to any proposition whatever. For suppose that p was merely contingently true. Then if at any time there were a person a who was mistaken about p then the following conjunction would be true: p & Map which of course is p & Bap & $\sim p$, which is a contradiction!

But of course all that follows from this is the truism that one cannot believe mistakenly any proposition which happens to be true, which does not mean that one cannot have a mistaken belief *about* it (i.e. regard it to be false). In short what one is capable of doing is, to believe mistakenly of a proposition which is false (contingently or necessarily) that it is true, and conversely to believe of a proposition which is true (contingently or necessarily) that it is false. In other words, what Descartes maintains is that it is possible that in a situation in which p is the case that nevertheless Ma $\sim p$ and conversely in a situation in which $\sim p$ is the case Map is true and this creates no problems for (*UPE*).

However the real objection to (*UPE*) is the one we brought against certain attempts in the previous chapter to define fallibilism, namely, that it employs the irrelevant notion of logical possibility which can be of no help in the present context. Map merely states that error is logically possible, that is, that there is no formal contradiction between $\sim p$ and the statement that a believes that p. But to say this is to say something that is entirely beyond dispute and devoid of interest. To put it differently, $(p)(a)\Diamond Map$ says that every one is mistaken about everything in at least one possible world, and that is compatible with holding that nobody is mistaken about anything in the actual world. Strangely enough therefore (*UPE*) not only fails to express total scepticism but is even compatible with absolute omniscience!

One might attempt to salvage the core of (UPE) by quantifying existentially over propositions in the actual world, and thus advance:

$$(UPE^*) \quad (a)(\exists p)Map.$$

This expression turns out however to be entirely inadequate as it is far too weak and at the same time, in a certain sense, too strong as a statement of scepticism. It is compatible with a doctrine of nearly perfect cognitivism according to which our methods of inquiry are so highly reliable that we know everything we claim to know with the sole exception of a single proposition. On the other hand it may also be contended that (UPE^*) is too strong since even the most radical sceptic does not go as far as to insist that some of our well supported beliefs are decidedly false. For all he knows each one of those be true. Except that if this should indeed be the case then we happen to be very lucky since there is just no guarantee that any of our beliefs is actually true. The reason why we know absolutely nothing is not because all or some of our 'justified' beliefs are downright false but because none of them are *really* justified.

Section 2

The groundlessness of our beliefs

In the fourth section of their paper Griffin and Harton advance

$$(14) \quad (p)(a) \sim JBap$$

as a candidate for adequately representing the sceptical position. However, they find is objectionable:[2]

> Beliefs are justified when there is evidence to support them (and none against), but this evidence does not have to be conclusive, nor to ensure that the belief is certain or immune to revision. Indeed, even false beliefs (e.g. Newton's belief in the theory of gravitation) may be justified (i.e. supported by the best available evidence). If such cases of false but justified beliefs were *not* possible we would have no need to state $Kap \rightarrow p$ as a separate condition of knowledge since the fact that a belief was justified would ensure its truth.

This objection seems to be off target. Let me begin by distinguishing two major versions of scepticism. On the first version there is no knowledge without absolute certainty, and since absolute certainty is unobtainable, there is no knowledge. On the second version the justification that is sufficient for providing knowledge need not guarantee truth, it is merely one that establishes the credibility of a given proposition to a high enough degree so as to place it beyond reasonable doubt. However, it is never the case that we succeed in doing even this much.

It appears that what Griffin and Harton have said does not affect the latter version of scepticism. According to this version it may be asserted that

$$(\alpha) \quad \phi ap \leftrightarrow JBap$$

with ϕap for 'a has verified p by method ϕ' and ϕ is a superior method of verification not available in practice. Yet ϕ is not a perfect method and therefore it is still the case that (β) $\phi ap \nleftrightarrow p$ and hence (γ) $JBap \nleftrightarrow p$ as demanded by Griffin and Harton. But since as we have said ϕ is not available in practice (δ) $(p)(a) \sim \phi ap$. Now the two expressions (α) and (δ) yield (14) $(p)(a) \sim JBap$.

But their objection does not seem very effective even against the first version. Surely the mere statement of the denial of scepticism amounts to no reason why scepticism is untenable. Given that the core of the sceptical position is that no evidence can secure anything with complete certainty and that there is no knowledge without certainty, then the simple proclamation of the opposite, namely, that 'evidence does not have to be conclusive, nor to ensure that the belief is certain or immune to revision' amounts to no argument and thus provides no good reason why scepticism cannot be entertained.

It is also somewhat difficult to see what was the point of mentioning that, in the conditions for knowledge, the truth of p constitutes an extra requirement beside $JBap$. It must be obvious to all that the theory of knowledge has been developed by people who held that knowledge was possible and therefore the conditions required for obtaining it were of genuine interest. In other words, those who made it their business to study the foundations, justification and scope of knowledge were bound to believe in its existence, i.e. were non-sceptics. Thus the definition of 'knowledge', which is the main pillar of epistemology may be assumed to have been formulated by so-called cognitivists, who unlike sceptics, did not hold that $JBap \rightarrow p$. There cannot be much point in using the definition of knowledge offered by cognitivists as evidence against the sceptical position the very essence of which is the denial of the validity of that definition.

It seems reasonable therefore to conclude that $(p)(a) \sim JBap$ is an adequate formal expression of the essential grounds underlying scepticism, where the universe of discourse depends on the scope of one's doubt. Thus for example, for someone whose misgivings are rooted in his lack of confidence in the method of induction, p ranges over conclusions of inductive reasoning, and so on.

Section 3

The positive distortion of our beliefs

In a remarkable and well known paper Keith Lehrer has defended an all-embracing kind of scepticism and claims that there isn't anything that he knows to be true. His lack of knowledge extends over even his lack of knowledge, that is, he does not know even that he does not know anything, in spite of the fact that many propositions seem quite obviously true to him : he cannot rule out the possibility that there may be some highly intelligent malevolent beings in outer space who are manipulating his brain so that false propositions look true to him.[3]

Lehrer's approach could be seen as an improvement on Descartes' demon argument as it makes no recourse to anything supernatural and is based on theories that were quite unimagined in the seventeenth century. Descartes had no idea how vast the universe is, that our own galaxy is only one in a hundred billion, that a single average galaxy has over a hundred billion stars in it and an even larger number of planets. According to the best astronomical thinking today the probability is very high that life, with greatly varying intelligence, is common throughout the universe.

I should like to mention in passing that I do not claim to understand Lehrer's argument in support of his contention that his scepticism encompasses also the knowledge of his own sensation. He maintains for instance that he cannot know that he is in pain :[4]

How could this happen? It might happen either because of some general belief, to wit, that itches are pains, which one has been led to believe to by some authority, or one may simply be misled on this occasion because one has been told by some authority that one will experience pain.

Now admittedly when for instance I am experiencing an intense toothache I may have no way of telling whether it is due to a decaying tooth or that actually nothing is wrong with my teeth and the excruciating pain has been induced by someone hypnotically convincing me of its existence. But the very fact that I cannot tell the difference shows that the two experiences are indistinguishable. Thus it is very hard to understand what sense there is in telling me, 'It may not be actually true that you are now having a crushingly unpleasant experience' when my 'mere belief' that I do have such an experience feels precisely as crushingly unpleasant as 'actually' having it.

Let us ignore this problem and inquire into the exact nature of Lehrer's argument. Risto Hilpinen has in a very illuminating recent paper made explicit the presuppositions on the basis of which it is possible to arrive with the use of elementary epistemic logic at the required conclusion.[5] He calls the hypothesis that there exist extra-terrestrial tricksters *the sceptical hypothesis* or briefly *s*. If *Eh* means that *h* (which is a basic hypothesis) is completely justified for a person *a*, then it is reasonable to assert:

$$(\textbf{\textit{L1}}) \quad s \rightarrow \sim Eh.$$

In addition Hilpinen supposes:

$$(\textbf{\textit{S2}}) \quad \sim E \sim s$$

thus not assuming that Lehrer would go as far as claiming it justified to believe *s*; all we do is ascribe to him the view that one is not justified in maintaining positively that *s* is false. He then enunciates a general theorem:

$$(\textbf{\textit{S3}}) \quad \text{If } p \rightarrow q, \text{ then } \sim E \sim p \rightarrow \sim E \sim q.$$

I should like to point out that if *E* means the same as our *JB* then (*S3*) is not well founded. It is after all possible for *a* not to realise that $p \rightarrow q$ and also correctly establish that $\sim E \sim p$ and on the basis of false evidence (but not being in the position to suspect the falsity of the evidence) arrive at the justified belief that $\sim q$. However if *E* stands for our *JB** ((cf. Chapter One) i.e. 'objectively speaking it can be established on the basis of information in *a*'s possession') then it seems that the validity of (*S3*) has to be conceded.

Now Hilpinen reconstructs Lehrer's proof formally as follows:

(1)	$s \rightarrow \sim Eh$	(*L1*)
(2)	$\sim E \sim s$	(*S2*)
(3)	If $s \rightarrow \sim Eh$, then $\sim E \sim s \rightarrow \sim E \sim \sim Eh$	(*S3*) $s/p, \sim Eh/q$
(4)	$\sim E \sim s \rightarrow \sim E \sim \sim Eh$	(1) & (3) *Modus Ponens*
(5)	$\sim EEh$	(2) & (4) *Modus Ponens*
(6)	$\sim EEh \rightarrow \sim Eh$	

(6) is the contrapositive of (*L2*), the principle that if *a* is justified in believing that *h* then he is also justified in believing that he is justified in believing that *h*, i.e. $Eh \rightarrow EEh$.

(7)	$\sim Eh$	(5) & (6) *Modus Ponens*

It should be pointed out that some would refuse to concede that $Eh \rightarrow EEh$, and hence deny the validity of (6). It really depends on the view they would take on the question touched upon in Chapter Two concerning a person who establishes the acidity of a liquid with the help of a litmus paper without being able to justify his use of this method. The crucial question is: what happens when *a* is able to provide rational grounds for his belief in *h* by citing the positive results of what happens to be a universally regarded reliable test T for ascertaining the truth of h, but cannot provide grounds for his holding that T is in fact a trustworthy test for establishing h? Some would hold that in such case a would be justified in believing that h but not in believing that Eh, i.e. Eh would be true but not EEh, contrary to what Hilpinen says. We have to bear in mind therefore that Hilpinen's derivation works only according to those who maintain that in order to justify one's belief in h it is necessary also to justify one's belief in the validity of one's justification of h.

Now Hilpinen himself expresses misgivings about the previous derivation but for different reasons. He believes that premise ($S2$) is highly questionable. Hilpinen claims that Lehrer's defence of ($S2$) is based on the following principle:

(ϕ) A hypothesis may be rejected as unjustified only if it is possible to present a convincing argument against it.

Hilpinen suggest that it does seem possible to present an argument against s and consequently (ϕ) does not warrant the assertibility of $\sim E \sim s$. The argument is based on the assumed special nature of basic beliefs which may be regarded as self-warranting. But later on page 171 he concedes that his argument will not convince the sceptic who holds a different view about the nature of basic beliefs.

It seems to me that a much more conclusive objection can be raised against Lehrer's argument, one which does not presuppose any particular views concerning basic beliefs and one which without questioning the validity of (ϕ) demonstrates its uselessness or at any rate it shows that without some extra substantial principle concerning how to adjudicate between conflicting hypotheses—a principle that by no means seems easy to come by—Principle (ϕ) is of no help in allowing us to derive the sceptical conclusion Hilpinen thought one may arrive at.

In the argument that follows I too shall be using elementary epistemic logic only. I shall introduce however a somewhat trivial theorem not employed before, namely:

$$(L2^*) \quad \sim Eh \to E \sim Eh.$$

I do not believe that anyone should wish to maintain that ($L2^*$) is less reasonable than ($L2$). After all if the information that a possesses is such that objectively speaking a is unjustified in holding h then it can be shown that this is so.

Now Lehrer has introduced the hypotheses of the existence of very powerful creatures who prevent us from forming correct beliefs and accordingly claimed that $\sim E \sim s$, simply because we have no positive proof that $\sim s$. He will then surely not object to us entertaining the thought that perhaps even more powerful creatures exist as well who happen to be benevolent and disapprove of the mischievous machinations of the relatively weak creatures and make sure that their evil designs are completely frustrated. Since it is reasonable to assume that there are no positive arguments that show our hypothesis to be less likely than Lehrer's we may assert: $\sim E \sim t$ **(T2)** where t denotes our story concerning those benevolent super-beings. Also it seems that we may assert $t \rightarrow Eh$ since the truth of t means that all the interferences of the malevolent beings are nullified. Thus we have:

(1′)	$t \rightarrow Eh$		
(2′)	$\sim E \sim t$	**(T2)**	
(3′)	If $t \rightarrow Eh$ then $\sim E \sim t \rightarrow \sim E \sim Eh$	**(S3)**	$t/p,\ Eh/q$
(4′)	$\sim E \sim t \rightarrow \sim E \sim Eh$	(1) & (3) M. P.	
(5′)	$\sim E \sim Eh$	(2) & (4) M. P.	
(6′)	$\sim E \sim h \rightarrow Eh$	**(L2*)** Contraposition	
(7′)	Eh	(5) & (6) M. P.	

which contradicts (7).

One way of resolving the contradiction between (7) and (7′) would be to say that **(L1)** $(s \rightarrow \sim Eh)$ was not valid. After all given the conjunction of s and t which implies the foiling of the attempts to interfere with our beliefs, the truth of s does not rule out the truth of Eh. Thus **(L1)** is valid only if it is reasonable to assume that t is false, i.e. that $E \sim t$. But by the principle Hilpinen attributes to Lehrer, Principle (ϕ), one seems to be entitled to postulate t no less than s; Principle (ϕ) may therefore be said to prohibit us from rejecting t in the absence of some positive reason for doing so and hence **(L1)** is seen to be invalid. But if we are not allowed to maintain **(L1)** then (7) cannot be derived. This then results in the elimination of the contradiction as well as in the invalidation of Lehrer's sceptical hypothesis.

The only way to attempt to revive the threat of Lehrer's creatures is by insisting that (ϕ) being an entirely general principle it applies not only to s but also to s^*, namely:

There exist extra-terrestrial tricksters who are *not* frustrated in their efforts to subvert all our knowledge-claims.

Clearly, (ϕ) does not apply to the conjunction s^* & t since that conjunction is contradictory and thus 'it is possible to present a convincing argument against it'. In other words (ϕ) can apply either to s^* & t or to $\sim s^*$ & t and absolutely no guidance has been provided as to which it is to be taken to apply. Nothing has been said that would point toward s^* & t rather than toward $\sim s^*$ & t hence (ϕ) is of no use in giving us the vital premise required for the derivation of Lehrer's sceptical conclusion.

It should be mentioned that Descartes dream argument reviewed in the first chapter has the advantage of not running into such difficulties. The legitimacy of entertaining the possibility of our dreaming is not grounded merely in a principle like (ϕ). Descartes has explicitly argued that there are good positive reasons for maintaining that it is unjustifiable to declare the hypothesis that he is dreaming to be false, namely, his past experience. Often in the past he has woken up to find himself lying in bed and not actually partaking in any of the adventures he seemed to have so vividly experienced partaking in a moment earlier. Lehrer of course could not claim to draw on any such evidence. Modern astronomy may have confirmed the high likelihood of intelligent extraterrestrial beings, but whether these are benevolent or not or, if they are of both kinds, which sort is more powerful (so that their designs prevail over us) is something about which we have not got the slightest clue.

Before concluding let me mention that Lehrer is wise enough to realise that many may suspect that he is not really serious in his advocacy of thorough-going scepticism. After all people may well argue that he could not have become the highly successful academic he in fact is, were it not that he made very good use of everything he has learnt from experience concerning the effective way of managing one's affairs. He attempts to disarm his critics by explaining that although we know absolutely nothing this need not prevent us from getting along quite well in the world without assigning any certainty to any proposition but by assigning merely probabilities to them. It is extremely hard to see what point Lehrer is trying to make here. According to his conclusion while he does not know that bread nourishes he assigns high probability to it doing so. But he will surely admit that, since there isn't a single thing he knows to be the case, he does not *know* that it is highly probable that bread nourishes, he merely believes that it is. But then there is absolutely no reason why he should not maintain something more; nothing prevents him from asserting that he believes it to be a certainty that bread nourishes. After all the scepticism he advocates, as he himself made very clear, does not prevent him from believing anything; it only prevents him from knowing anything. Thus there does not seem to be any point in introducing probabilities.

5

Justified Belief and Probability

Section 1

The role of probabilities in epistemic logic

As we have seen in Chapter Three, beliefs may be justified to different degrees. In this chapter we shall examine some of the important implications of the view held by many that the degree to which a belief is justified for an individual a is determined by the probability of that belief in the context of a's other relevant justified beliefs. The simple apparatus of elementary probability theory can therefore be put to good use in the investigation of the status of various claims concerning the logical relations among justified beliefs. The axioms of probability theory may thus be looked upon as forming a part of the system of elementary epistemic logic. We may begin by illustrating this point by a relatively simple example involving the contention we have assumed in Chapter Four to be true, namely,

$$(S3) \quad \text{If } p \to q \text{ then } \sim E \sim p \to \sim E \sim q$$

where as we shall recall E is brief for JB^* or 'the objective situation is such that one is justified in believing that'.

Let me proceed to show how $(S3)$ may be derived with the use of elementary probability theory. First of all we note that Ep amounts to the claim that a belief in p is justified to at least the degree that is sufficient to render it rational to sucscribe to p, and anyone who does subscribe to p (with p being true), may be regarded as having the knowledge that p. Without entering into any inquiry about what its precise value may be, it is obvious that there is some fraction n the value of which lies between $\frac{1}{2}$ and 1, and Ep iff $Pr(p) \geqslant n$, that is a belief in p is justified, if and only if, the probability of p equals at least n.

Now there is well known theorem which states

$$(a) \quad \text{If } p \to q \text{ then } Pr(p) \leqslant Pr(q).$$

The validity of this theorem can be argued for informally by saying that if p logically implies q then p must be asserting at least as much as q and in general even more. But clearly a larger claim, will, if anything, be less, and certainly not more probable, than the more modest claim.

Now let us prove $(S3)$:

(1)	$p \to q$	Assumption
(2)	$Pr(p) \leqslant Pr(q)$	(1) & (a), *Modus Ponens*
(3)	$Pr(\sim p) > Pr(\sim q)$	(2) & Given that $Pr(\sim p) = 1 - Pr(p)$
(4)	$\sim E \sim (p) \to \sim E(\sim q)$	(3) & Transitivity of '$<$'.

(that is, from the definition of E it follows that

$$E \sim p = Pr(\sim p) \geqslant n$$

negating both sides:

$$\sim E \sim p = \sim [Pr(\sim p) \geqslant n]$$
$$= Pr(\sim p) < n \quad \text{(call this } \phi\text{)}.$$

But by (3) $Pr(\sim q)$ is *less* than $Pr(\sim p)$ and by (ϕ) $Pr(\sim p)$ is *less* than n hence $Pr \sim (q)$ is certainly less than n and thus $\sim E \sim q)$

$$(5) \quad \text{If } p \to q \text{ then } \sim E \sim (p) \to \sim E \sim (q)$$

by Conditional Proof (1)–(4). Q.E.D.

Section 2

Some counterintuitive results of probability theory

The reason why it is of particular importance to make use of the elementary formalism of probability theory in our investigations of justified belief is that the assessment of probabilities is a notoriously slippery affair, and many quite elementary statements which may look obviously true when considered commonsensically unaided by rigorous derivation turn out to be false when examined formally. C S Peirce referring to probability, for example, said 'This branch of mathematics is the only one, I believe, in which good writers frequently get results entirely erroneous'. Lately some very interesting work has been done by K ahneman and Tversky attempting to categorise various types of misconceptions involving probabilities which they claim are systematic and even predictable.[1] In this section I shall present three examples where we find that results that commonsense yields clash with those obtained through more rigorous reasoning. There are more such examples but these three are of special significance. In the next chapter we shall discuss a few problems that have recently puzzled a considerable number of philosophers and it will turn out that we shall be able to make good use of these examples which will help us to achieve the clarification needed for the solution of those problems.

Example 1:   Suppose it is given that $E(A/B \lor C)$ which means 'belief that A is justified, given that either B or C is true'. Can we infer from this that both $E(A/B)$ and $E(A/C)$ are true? In other words is the expression

$$E(A/B \lor C) \rightarrow E(A/B) \ \& \ E(A/C)$$

a theorem of epistemic logic?

On a commonsense view it looks highly plausible to claim that when we are given that $E(A/B \lor C)$ we are virtually also given both $E(A/B)$ and $E(A/C)$. The disjunction $B \lor C$ is true when merely B is true as well as when C alone is true. Therefore translated into English, $E(A/B \lor C)$ seems to assert explicitly that belief in A is justified as soon as B alone is known to be true and again when nothing but C is given as true. Retranslating into symbols, what we just said amounts to affirming that $E(A/B \lor C)$ is equivalent to asserting the conjunction of $E(A/B)$ and $E(A/B)$.

There seems to be also many concrete examples to support the argument for the validity of the expression in question. Suppose for instance that

B: A reliable person b testifies that A is true

C: A reliable person c testifies that A is true.

Clearly the expression $E(A/B \lor C)$ says that we are justified in believing A either on the testimony of b alone or the testimony of c alone. This means that either of these two people is reliable to the degree that his testimony uncorroborated by any extra evidence is sufficient to make A justified. This amounts to saying that $E(A/B \lor C)$ logically implies $E(A/B) \ \& \ E(A/C)$.

Surprisingly enough we get different results when we examine the matter with the aid of the elementary formalism of the theory of probability. There are a number of ways to proceed but the easiest to follow, one which makes matters practically visible to the eye, is by using simple diagrams: see Fig. 1.

The elliptical figure C contains 4 sample-points 2 of which are A's. Thus *in C* the frequency of A's is $\frac{2}{4}$ or $\frac{1}{2}$. This corresponds to the likelihood that if we select something from C it will turn out to be an A. That is $Pr(A/C) = \frac{1}{2}$.

The union of B and C contains 12 sample-points, 9 of which are A's. Thus in $B \cup C$ the frequency of A's is $\frac{9}{12}$ or $\frac{3}{4}$. This means that $Pr(A/B \lor C) = \frac{3}{4}$.

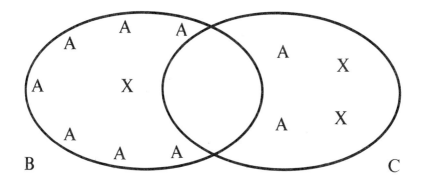

Let us postulate that $E(p)$ iff $Pr(p) \geq \frac{3}{4}$. It follows then that $E(A/B \vee C)$, however, $\sim E(A/C)$.

Here we have an example where $E(A/B \vee C)$ is true, yet $E(A/C)$ is false. Clearly therefore it is *not* the case that $E(A/B \vee C)$ entails both $E(A/B)$ and $E(A/C)$.

To see clearly why this is, indeed *that* this is how it should be, it is best to look at a concrete example. Suppose dimes are being collected at a party held at the Townhouse. In the small hall 20 US dimes and 20 Canadian dimes are collected while at the main hall 70 US dimes and 10 Canadian dimes are collected. Later the contents of the collection-boxes are transferred into a third box. Let

A = The coin drawn at random from a collection made at the town party is a US dime

B = The coin drawn belongs to the collection made in the main hall

C = The coin drawn belongs to the collection made in the small hall

Clearly if the draw is made from the box into which all the coins are ultimately transferred, in which there are 90 US dimes and only 30 Canadian dimes, then the probability of getting a US coin is $\frac{90}{120}$ which is $\frac{3}{4}$ and therefore $E(A/B \vee C)$ may be regarded to hold. On the other hand if we draw a coin earlier from the collection box that has been used in the small hall there is only 50–50 chance for drawing a US coin and therefore $E(A/C)$ is definitely false. This therefore serves to illustrate how $E(A/B \vee C)$ is compatible with the falsity of at least one of the conjuncts $E(A/B)$ and $E(A/C)$.

It should be obvious that Fig. 1 may be taken to represent this story if B and C represent the main hall and small hall respectively, (and each A is 10 US dimes while each X is 10 Canadian dimes).

Example 2:   Now we shall consider the question: if it is given that $\sim E$ $(\sim B/A)$ can we infer that $E(B \supset C/A) \supset (C/A \,\&\, B)$? In other words is

$$\sim E(\sim B/A) \to [E(B \supset C/A) \supset E(C/A \,\&\, B)]$$

a theorem of epistemic logic?

Once more judged by commonsense alone the verdict will be that we have here a valid theorem. As we know $B \supset C$ is true when either B is false or C is true. We are however assured that $\sim E(\sim B/A)$, i.e. that it is not reasonable to regard B to be false (given that A), and therefore it follows that if $B \supset C$ is nevertheless true, it is reasonable to assume that this is so because C is true (when both A and B are true). We have thus clearly stated that, when given both A and B, we are justified in believing that C. In other words we have demonstrated that if $\sim E(\sim B/A)$, then if $E(B \supset C)$, we may infer $E(C/A \,\&\, B)$.

There is even a way in which one might argue for the same conclusion and of which one might easily become convinced that it actually amounts to a rigorous formal proof. There is a well known elementary law of logic called the Law of Exportation which says:

$$(A \,\&\, B) \supset C \equiv A \supset (B \supset C).$$

Now it does not follow that when the left hand side of the above is highly probable then of necessity $Pr(C/A \lor B)$ is of high value since the probability of the former may equal one simply because B is false. However given that $\sim E(\sim B/A)$ then if the right hand side is highly probable then the value of $Pr(A/B \lor C)$ may also be assumed to be high and thus $E(A/B \lor C)$.

Now let us examine this matter with the aid of the highly illuminating method used earlier: see Fig. 2.

Let the union of A and B represent the entire sample space and therefore the shaded area of A stands for $\sim B$. Thus $\sim B$ contains 9 sample points. Only one of the C's is contained in A. Figure A contains 12 points of which 9 are members of the union of $\sim B$ and C. Hence the frequency of $\sim B \cup C$ *in* A is $\frac{10}{12} = \frac{5}{6}$. This means that

$$Pr(\sim B \lor C/A) = \tfrac{5}{6} > \tfrac{3}{4}.$$

The intersection of A and B contains 3 sample-points one of which is C. Thus the frequency of C's in $A \cap B$ is $\frac{1}{3}$. Therefore $Pr(C/A \,\&\, B) = \frac{1}{3} < \frac{3}{4}$.

Remembering that $\sim B \lor C$ is logically equivalent to $B \supset C$ we conclude that $Pr(B \supset C/A) > \frac{3}{4}$ and therefore $E(B \supset C)$ is true, while $E(C/A \,\&\, B)$ is false.

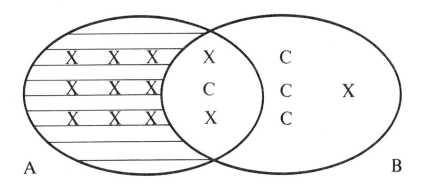

Once more we see that commonsense is not a reliable guide in matters like these.

Example 3:   This example involves a result known as Simpson's Paradox that is important enough to bear the name of the British statistician who first wrote about it in 1951.[2] It concerns the very basic and common assumption that evidence is accumulative. It is taken to be a universal principle that if evidence *e* supports a hypothesis *h* and likewise *f* supports it too, then the combination of *e* and *f* provides *h* even greater support. Therefore if *Eah* follows from an individual *a* having *e* alone as well as from his having *f* alone then it seems beyond question that in case *a* has both *e* and *f* then *Eah* applies with even greater force. Simpson has however shown with the aid of results obtained in the testing of a new treatment for a certain disease that this need not always be the case.

Considerably less space will be taken up if I do not go into the details of Simpson's experiment and give instead a straightforward and brief illustration of the very same idea. The reader will find no difficulties in constructing any number of similar examples. Let

h = Fred murdered Smith

e = *x*, *y*, and *z*, highly respected pillars of the community testify to having seen Fred stab Smith on Monday morning and burning the body.

It should be agreed that $E(h/e)$ since *h* is likely to be regarded very highly likely to be true given the testimony of three greatly trusted citizens.

Similarly of course if

> f: u, v, and w, highly respected pillars of the community testify to having seen Fred shoot Smith on Tuesday evening and dumping the body into the ocean

h is to be regarded as likely to be true as under the previous conditions, i.e. $E(h/f)$. At the same time, however, it is quite clear that $\sim E(h/e\,\&\,f)$ simply because when given both e and f together then we have witnesses at least three of whom are definitely liars and any reasonable jury would reject the testimony of all of them.

Section 3

A paradoxical result

Let us consider the story of Fred who was not permitted to be on the athletic team representing his college in the forthcoming sports events. The coach explained to a very disappointed Fred that the only reason why he cannot join the team is because he is overweight. A few weeks before the competitions are to take place Fred notices an advertisement concerning a weight-loss pill guaranteed to make anyone lose 20 lb in seven days. The ad includes several signed testimonies by people from all walks of life and there is a money-back guarantee to anyone not fully satisfied. Under the circumstances Fred is justified in believing that the pill will work for him. We may compile the following list of true propositions:

(1)   The hypothesis that the pill will cause Fred to lose considerable weight in a short period of time, is justified.

(2)   The hypothesis that if the pill works for Fred then he will be permitted to join the team, is justified.

(3)   If it should turn out that the pill does not work for Fred, then the hypothesis that he is not going to be permitted to join the team, is justified.

(4)   The pill in fact does not work.

I do not believe anyone would hesitate to admit that propositions (1)–(4) are definitely consistent and could therefore jointly be true. However let us look at the matter more closely. Let w be 'The pill works for Fred', and let t be 'Fred is permitted to join the team'. Then we may represent the four propositions symbolically:

(1a) $E(w)$ (assuming the probability of w to be $\frac{3}{4}$)

(2a) $E(w \supset t)$ (postulating that $Pr(w \supset t) = \frac{3}{4}$)

(3a) $\sim w \supset E(\sim t)$
(4a) $\sim w.$

Now we shall be able to derive the rather surprising result that as a matter of fact our four propositions are inconsistent.

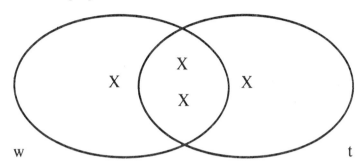

Suppose w contains 3 sample points, while the entire sample space has 4 such points. Thus $Pr(w) = \frac{3}{4}$, i.e. $E(w)$ in compliance with (1a).

The union of $\sim w$ and t also contains 3 sample-points. Thus $Pr(\sim w \lor t)$ $= \frac{3}{4} = Pr(w \supset t)$ and hence $E(w \supset t)$ in compliance with (2a).

At the same time, clearly, $Pr(t) = \frac{3}{4}$ and hence $E(t)$.

Thus we see that it is possible to have a situation in which $E(t)$ is true when both (1a) and (2a) hold. On the other hand (3a) and (4a) by *Modus Ponens* yield $E(\sim t)$. This amounts to a contradiction, since we know that $Pr(t) + Pr(\sim t) = 1$ and thus we cannot have the values of both the probabilities of t and $\sim t$ be higher than $\frac{1}{2}$.

The source of this paradoxical result is to be traced to our putting down (2a) which would quite commonly be recognised as an illegitimate step. Proposition (2) of course implies that the probability of 'if w then t' is of certain value but this is not equivalent to saying that $Pr(w \supset t)$ is of such value since the latter is one even when w is false, whereas the statement 'if the pill works for Fred then he will be permitted to join our team' will not be regarded as true as soon as it is given that the pill does not work. The correct expression to substitute for (2a), is $E(t/w)$. It is easily seen that if we have the correct symbolisation for (2) nothing paradoxical can be derived.

The paradox and its solution is of no great significance on its own. In the next chapter however we shall encounter a famous paradox advanced some years ago by R Chisholm that has aroused considerable amount of discussion. I hope to show there that we can put to good use what we have learned in this section concerning the apparent inconsistency among propositions (1)–(4) in order to discover the solution to Chisholm's paradox.

Section 4

Some elementary errors involving probabilities

As we have mentioned probability theory is a tricky subject and therefore it is not surprising to find even more elementary mistakes being committed than those discussed in the last section. Let us look briefly at some instructive examples.

Example 1   Let $p > q$ denote the counterfactual 'if p were true then q would be true'; then the question has been raised by J Tlumak and S Shuger whether $(Kp \ \& \ q) \supset \sim(Kq > \sim Kp)$ is a valid theorem of epistemic logic? This question, the authors explain amounts to asking whether knowledge would survive any of its extensions, that is, if a knows that p can we assume that a would still know that p no matter what other knowledge he attained? They contend that the above formula does not represent a valid theorem. It is possible, and even likely, that a given person exhausts his brain's real capacity for knowledge without coming to know every truth. Consequently a certain person might know that p while there are other propositions which are such that if he knew them, then he would not be capable of also knowing that p.[3]

We may note in passing that the point about someone completely exhausting his brain's capacity is, to say the least, very strange. Filling the brain up to its brim is such an out of the way phenomenon and furthermore it is something that has no real relevance to the nature of knowledge but only to the physical nature of the brain. Consequently it seems that when formulating epistemic theorems philosophers take it for granted that every assertion is made on the assumption that we are dealing with what happens under accustomed circumstances. To cite concrete evidence in support of my contention let us look at the well known debate concerning what is known as the KK-thesis. The advocates of the thesis have maintained that the expression $(a)(p)(Kap \supset KaKap)$ is a theorem of epistemic logic. Those who disagree do so because they feel that even though Kap amounts to the assertion that $p \ \& \ Bap \ \& \ JBap$, this does not guarantee the truth of every one of the nine conjuncts that are required to ensure that $KaKap$ is true. In particular the truth of the conjunct $BaJBap$ may seem not necessarily to follow. But if the point of our authors were correct then there would be a different reason why everyone should deny the KK-thesis. Surely there has to exist a case where Kap may be true while $KaKap$ cannot be true as when p is the very last true proposition for which there is room left in a's brain to be accommodated. At the very moment at which the knowledge of p is acquired a's brain reaches its saturation point and is no longer capable of assimilating even the most obvious information. It seems therefore that when dealing with the theorems of epistemic logic philosophers should disregard the physical idiosyncracies of the brain.

What is really remarkable is that although the authors declare that the formula purported to express the extendability thesis is 'clearly mistaken' because of such questionable reasons, they ignore what is an undoubtedly valid and very important reason why the formula must be rejected. What I am referring to is the point that often the evidence in our possession is misleading and causes us justifiably to believe what in fact is false. As a consequence, situations may arise (to which brief reference was made in Chapter One) where we may know less by knowing more. Let me give an example. Suppose I am not aware of the existence of black swans and shortly after arriving in Australia I decide to visit a small lake which I am told is inhabited by swans. Let us take

p: The swans on the lake I am about to visit are white.
q: The great majority of swans in Australia are black.

Given my limited background knowledge, I assume p to be true and may well be thought justified in my belief. Now it so happens that p is in fact true since the swans of this particular lake are not native to Australia; they have been imported from Europe. It is clearly therefore the case that Kp; i.e. I know that p. Now consider what would happen if I were to learn of the truth of q. Surely in that case I would be likely no longer to believe that p, and even if I would continue to believe I certainly should cease to be justified in doing so (since I am completely ignorant of the special way in which the swans came to populate the lake). Thus even though we have here Kp nevertheless $Kq > \sim Kp$. Thus we have demonstrated the falsity of the formula under consideration on the basis of purely epistemological factors.

Example 2 In a paper 'Some Epistemic Implications of "Crucial Experiments"' Philip Quinn denotes 'p is beyond reasonable doubt' by 'Rp' which he also defines as $BpPWp$ meaning 'it is epistemically preferable to believe that p than to withhold one's belief that p'. He then goes onto enunciate several theorems involving the operator R. One of these is:

$$(P1)\quad [Rp \ \& \ Rq \ \& \ \vdash((p \ \& \ q) \supset r)] \supset Rr^4$$

which may look reasonable and virtually ensured to be valid by *Modus Ponens*.

Now, of course, since Rp means that p's credibility is high so much so that beyond reasonable doubt we may assume that $Rp \leftrightarrow Pr(p) \geqslant k$ where k is above $\frac{1}{2}$. Given that both Rp and Rq then in the simplest case where p and q are independent $Pr(p \ \& \ q) \geqslant k^2$ from which we may only infer that

$Pr(r) \geqslant k^2$ and given that k is less than one, $k^2 < k$ and therefore it may well not be the case that Rr. So it is a relatively simple matter to see that $(P1)$ is not a valid theorem of epistemic logic.

Example 3 On page 63 of the same paper Quinn advances the following rule:

$(R1)$ In circumstances $R \sim (h \text{ \& } a)$, if Ra then $R \sim h$

$(R1)$ is of special significance to Quinn and he uses it to show that Duhem's famous thesis concerning the impossibility of falsifying a specific hypothesis is wrong. As we may recall, Duhem maintained that though a crucial experiment can establish that $R \sim (h \text{ \& } a)$, i.e. that since the observations are incompatible with what has been predicted on the basis of the hypothesis to be tested it follows only that the conjunction of that hypothesis and the auxiliary hypotheses a must be false, it does not establish anything further about the status of h or a. Quinn believes however that he has just shown this not always to be the case. He claims that in those cases in which it is legitimate to assume that Ra then since $R \sim (h \text{ \& } a)$ it follows that $R \sim h$.

However, it is easy to see that $(R1)$ is not valid. To facilitate matters let us set $k = \frac{3}{4}$ in which case

$$(\phi) \quad R \sim (h \text{ \& } a) \leftrightarrow Pr(\sim (h \text{ \& } a)) \geqslant \tfrac{3}{4}$$

but $Pr(\sim (h \text{ \& } a)) = 1 - Pr(h \text{ \& } a) = 1 - Pr(h) \cdot Pr(a)$ (h and a assumed independent). In view of Ra we shall let $Pr(a) = \frac{3}{4}$ and then $Pr(h) = \frac{1}{3}$ makes $1 - Pr(h) \cdot Pr(a) = \frac{3}{4}$ from which it follows that $R \sim (h \text{ \& } a)$ by (ϕ). But $Pr(\sim h) = 1 - Pr(h) = 1 - \frac{1}{3} = \frac{2}{3} < \frac{3}{4}$. Thus it is not the case that $R \sim h$! Therefore it follows that $(R1)$ is false.

Section 5

The notion of epistemic preferability

I shall now touch briefly on some further reasons why the axioms of probability should be regarded as constituting a part of epistemic logic by indicating the existence of other important points of contact between epistemic and probablistic concepts. As is well known R M Chisholm has developed an important approach to epistemic logic in which the central role is played by the notion of 'epistemic preferability'. For example one of the axioms of the system developed by Chisholm says: $(Bh \, P \, Bi) \equiv (B \sim i \, P \, B \sim h)$ which means, 'Belief in h is preferable to a belief in i if and only if, a belief in $\sim i$ is preferable to a belief in $\sim h$'. This axiom (and every other of his axioms) can be shown to be valid if we assume that 'x is epistemically preferable to y' means 'x is more probable than y'. In that case for example,

Bh P Bi translates into $Pr(h) > PR(i)$. Thus assuming that $Pr(h) = n$, we may then put $Pr(i) = n - \varepsilon$. It follows therefore that $Pr(\sim i) = 1 - n + \varepsilon$, while $Pr(\sim h) = 1 - n$. Clearly therefore $Pr(h) > Pr(i) \equiv Pr(\sim i) > Pr(\sim h)$ which is the mirror image of Chisholm's axiom.

I know of one philosopher who has insisted that the notion of *epistemic preferability* cannot be equated with any probability notion. Roy A Sorensen attempted to make this point by referring to a paper by Chisholm and Kiem (*Ratio*, 1972) in which they have advanced

$$(A_2) \quad (\sim(pPq) \,\&\, \sim(qPr)) \supset \sim(pPr)$$

(where *pPq* is brief for our *Bp P Bq*) as one of their axioms.[5] All agree that the probabilistic counterpart of (A_2) is a valid theorem but Sorensen believes that (A_2), which is the assertion of the transitivity of epistemic indifference, can be shown to be invalid. He begins his objection to (A_2) by asking us to suppose that

p_i The bucket containing water of the highest temperature of all k buckets is b_i.

It is conceivable that Jim who is trying to determine which of the buckets contains the hottest water should conclude that b_i and b_j are of equal temperature or that $\sim(p_i P p_j)$ since the actual temperature difference between b_i and b_j is too small for him to discern. For similar reason he also concludes that $\sim(p_j P p_k)$. However the temperature difference between b_i and b_k may be large enough for Jim to discern and he concludes that $(p_i P p_k)$. But the conjuction of these three results violates (A_2) and it shows that epistemic indifference is not transitive. Sorensen concludes his note:[6]

> The above argument also shows that epistemic preferability cannot be given a probabilistic interpretation. If '*pPq*' is read as '*p* is more probable than *q*' then the standard definition of indifference as $\sim(pPq) \,\&\, \sim(qPp)$ forces us to read '*pPq*' as '*p* and *q* are equiprobable'. It would then follow that the epistemic indifference relation is transitive. Since this relation has already been shown to be nontrasitive, the probabilistic interpretation of epistemic preferability must be rejected.

It seems however that (A_2) is a valid theorem of epistemic logic and that Sorensen's argument is involved in a simple error. Surely as soon as Jim information which forces him to conclude that, even though ne could not information which forces him to conclude that even though he could not feel it, b_i must be of some what higher temperature than b_j, since otherwise how is one to account for only b_i but not b_j feeling hotter than b_k? Thus while it is true that earlier it was legitimate to hold that $\sim(p_i P p_j)$, now in view of the latest observation involving the comparative felt temperatures of the last two buckets, plus elementary physics, Jim is obliged to change his beliefs. Thus at the time when it is justifiable for him to hold $\sim(p_iPp_j)$ it is not justifiable for him yet to hold (p_iPp_k), and thus we have no counterexample to (A_2); and at the time when it is justifiable for him to hold (p_iPp_k) then of course he can no longer justifiably hold $\sim(p_iPp_j)$.

Conceivably, however, some might wish to put up a defence on Sorensen's behalf. Given that $JBap$ is compatible with the falsity of p, there is considerable latitude as to what is to be taken as sufficiently justified. Consequently some might wish to advocate the thesis that what amounts to acceptable justification will vary with the knowledge and intellectual capacity of different individuals and that it is reasonable to apply less demanding standards to less gifted knowledge seekers. Thus our Jim might be assumed to be a conscientious but not too bright investigator who among other things believes himself to have an adequate knowledge of physics though in fact he was never capable of grasping some of the most basic notions of the theory of heat. He has given the matter all the thought that should be expected from him and yet failed to realise that objectively, bucket i must be the hottest. Thus even after discovering that (p_iPp_k) he continues to believe—and given his circumstances justifiably so—that $\sim(p_iPp_j)$ holds.

Regardless of the plausibility of such a highly relativistic view concerning warranted belief, what has just been said cannot reasonably be taken as Sorensen's defence. On the thesis of extreme relativism JB is determined differently for every individual, and it is impossible therefore to have any system of axioms for epistemic preferability. If we are willing to admit any absurd reasoning as long as it represents the honest best of a given individual every putative axiom is bound to be inapplicable to some persons. For example there will be individuals unable to figure out that $Bh\,P\,Bi$ entails and is entailed by $B\sim i\,P\,B\sim h$ and hence Chisholm's simpler axiom mentioned earlier does not necessarily hold either. The fact that (A_2) has specifically been singled out for criticism shows that Sorensen's position cannot be defended by invoking the thesis of extreme relativism.

Now that the issue has already been touched upon we might as well glance quickly at the question: who determines the standards of reasoning, deductive and inductive, to be used in assessing the warrantedness of beliefs? The answer seems to me, that these standards are determined by objective reality. We are of course fairly convinced that virtually all the rules of reasoning logicians and scientists subscribe to are sound, yet cannot entirely rule out the possibility that one or two of them are misconceived. If some of the rules of reasoning currently endorsed by the experts happens to be mistaken then this may eventually be realised and the rule be replaced; however, it also possible that it should go forever undetected.

The following passage suggests that not everyone might agree to what has just been said:[7]

It must be possible for there to be an epistemically perfect person. That is, it must be in principle possible for there to be an s and t such that s has no unjustified beliefs at t—Bst is included in Jst—and moreover as t changes s keeps Bst included in Jst by knowing the correct J-principles and having sufficiently strong will to adhere to them. . . . If this were not so, then the concept of justification would scarcely be coherent: the principles of justification would lay down a guide to forming and altering belief that even a person with a complete grasp of them and commitment to them, and with the best will in the world, might be unable to follow correctly. Any account of the moral justification of *action* that had the corresponding consequence would, clearly, have to be ruled unacceptable or else taken as showing that the notion of moral justification itself is incoherent and unacceptable. I see no reason why we should not say the same for the notion of justification of belief.

There are a number of things concerning this passage I am not quite certain about. For example I am not sure why we should be concerned only about the failure of a person who has a complete grasp of the correct rules but is unable for some reason to follow them properly and not also about a failure due to one's ignorance of the objectively adequate rules. However, I am fairly certain that the analogy between ethics and epistemology in the present context is misconceived. It may be said to be one of the most fundamental principles inherent in all reasonable ethical systems that no moral blame can be ascribed to an agent who is ignorant, for no fault of his own, that a given action is forbidden. Thus it is plausible to maintain that laying down even just a single moral rule that it is in principle unknowable to the individual upon whom the rule is supposed to be binding is to be involved in an inconsistency. It may well be claimed that it amounts to an 'immoral moral' rule in view of the fact that fairness itself is a basic moral value and it is immoral to make unfair demands on an individual.

The rules for establishing knowledge claims on the other hand, are impersonal; they are generated by the objective nature of reality with no regard to justice or fairness. Nature owes us nothing; we cannot insist that having exerted so much energy and taken so much care, we have earned the right that this or that belief of ours to be at least objectively highly probable. We should in fact consider ourselves highly lucky that we seem to have gotten so many of our beliefs right. There is absolutely no room for placing any reproach on anyone if some of our beliefs or even some of our methods for acquiring beliefs are faulty. Entertaining the possibility of such a fault does of course not amount to anything more devastating than having one more reason for subscribing to fallibilism.

6

Justified Beliefs and Obligations

Section 1

The central methodological rule of deontic logic

Some of the results of the last chapter are actually more important than they appear at first. This will become evident when we in this chapter see how they may be put to significant use in the construction of a solid basis for deontic logic. The reader may at first be wondering why a work said to be devoted to epistemology should contain a chapter not obviously related to the theory of knowledge. Soon however it will become clear that contrary to what one might have expected these two branches are very intimately interconnected. It will come as a surprise, and I trust as a rather pleasant surprise, to see that after the work of the last chapter, deontic logic, the development of which has been greatly hampered by a considerable number of problems and the difficulty of finding one's way among the unusually vast number of axiomatic systems proposed by different philosophers, can as a matter of fact be mastered almost without any effort at all. As we shall see we have already been provided with ready means for determining precisely what statements do and what statements do not constitute valid theorems in the logic of obligations as well as for resolving the various paradoxes and removing all the obstacles that have impeded the development of deontic logic.

R M Chisholm was the first person to note some time ago that there is a degree of similarity between empirical confirmation and ethical requirement; that epistemic and deontic logic share certain aspects with one another. He pointed out for instance that just as 'p confirms q' does not imply either that p occurs or that q occurs similarly 'p requires q' does not imply that p or q has actually taken place. Also confirmation (as well as rationally warranted belief) is defeasible and may be overridden with additional observation, and so is moral requirement.[1]

We shall see that Chisholm has merely touched upon the surface of something far reaching that is of utmost significance as well as usefulness. In fact the relation between the two logics is not merely very close but one can be said to be the full replica of the other. Because of this correspondence it can quickly be determined whether any theorem-like statement of deontic logic is or is not a valid theorem by examining its counterpart in epistemic logic to see whether the latter is or is not a valid theorem. In other words, the major advantage that results from the isomorphism between the two systems of applied logic is that instead of having to depend on intuition we are provided with a remarkably swift and fully effective method to determine whether any lawlike statement is or is not a valid theorem of deontic logic. This method requires that when confronted with a statement asserting that a certain set of deontic expressions implies another set and we wish to find out whether the statement represents a valid theorem, what we need is to change the operator 'O'—which stands for 'it is obligatory to see to it that . . .'—into the epistemic operator 'E' and see whether the resulting statement is or it not a valid theorem. Assuming that Eap^2 is determined by the probability of p for a then given that probability theory is more than 300 years old and that its basic features have long ago been clarified and are not subject to any controversy, the question whether a given sample statement concerning justified belief is or is not a valid theorem yields a quick and universally agreed answer.

Section 2

The first contrary-to-duty paradox

One type of difficulties that has greatly held back the development of deontic logic was the proliferation of paradoxes that have been symptomatic of a basic lack of proper understanding right from the inception of the whole new discipline. Aziza al-Hibri has in her useful, brief survey described no less than ten paradoxes formulated by different philosophers.[3]

We shall begin by looking at a paradox raised by Chisholm in 1963 and which has been described, recently, as the most famous and perhaps most worrisome paradox of Standard Deontic Logic by J W Decow, who is sceptical whether so far any adequate solution to it has been provided.[4]

Chisholm has pointed out the following four English sentences are intuitively consistent.

(1) It ought to be that a certain man go to the assistance of his neighbours.
(2) It ought to be that if he does go then he tell them he is coming.
(3) If he does not go then he ought not to tell them that he is coming.
(4) He does not go.

These sentences, however, are symbolised in standard deontic logic in the following manner:

(1a) Og	(3a) $\sim g \supset O \sim t$
(2a) $O(g \supset t)$	(4a) $\sim g$

Now (1a) and (2a) yield by the deontic distribution axiom, Ot, while (3a) and (4a) yield by *Modus Ponens* $O \sim t$. Thus it follows that both t and $\sim t$ are obligatory.

We notice at once that this paradox is the exact replica of the paradox we had in the previous chapter where we derived that both the belief that Fred is permitted to join the team and the belief that he is not permitted to do so are justified because highly probable. It is to be expected that the solutions are the same too. As in the context of Fred's story, same also in the case of Chisholm's (2), the correct symbolisation should be not $O(g \supset t)$ but rather $O(t/g)$. This crucial point was first recognised by von Wright. However, it so happens that in confirmation theory there would have been no room for hesitation to begin with since, as we have seen in the last chapter, there are conspicuous and entirely compelling reasons why 'the probability of t if g' is correctly represented by $Pr(t/g)$. Thus had the isomorphism between the two logics been recognised no paradox throwing a wrench into the smooth development of the formalisation of moral discourse would have arisen in the first place. In that case Chisholm's (2) would have been symbolised as $O(t/g)$. But then there would have been no way to derive $O(t)$ since as we shall see $O(g)$ & $O(t/g)$ does not imply $O(t)$.

Section 3

The second contrary-to-duty paradox

Contrary to what I have just stated, to many logicians it seemed that

$$(\alpha) \quad O(A/B) \mathrel{\&} O(B) \rightarrow O(A)$$

was a valid theorem of deontic logic. Van Fraasen, al-Hibri and David Lewis are among those who have adopted (α) as one of their basic axioms. On applying our principle however, it becomes evident at once that (α) cannot be regarded as a valid theorem. For by the Conjunctive Axiom:

$$(CA') \quad Pr(A/B) \cdot Pr(B) = Pr(A) \cdot Pr(B/A).$$

Clearly it is possible to have $Pr(A/B) = n$ as well as $Pr(B) = n$ and at the same time $Pr(A) < n$ while still satisfying (CA'). For as long as $Pr(B/A)$ is greater than n by a sufficiently large amount it may compensate for what is lacking in $Pr(A)$.[5] This means that it is possible to have $E(A/B)$ as well as

$E(B)$ and yet $E(A)$ does not obtain. In other words:

$$(\alpha^*) \quad E(A/B) \ \& \ E(B) \rightarrow E(A)$$

is not a valid theorem. It follows at once from our principle that the deontic counterpart of (α^*), namely (α), is not valid either.

Once we have established that (α) cannot be a valid theorem we are bound to find counter-examples, since now we shall be looking for such examples fully confident that they exist. And indeed such examples do exist. Suppose for instance

$A = $ I administer total anaesthetics to Fred
$B = $ I perform brain surgery on Fred who is my patient and requires urgently such an operation.

It may well be claimed that $O(A/B)$, since it should be quite inhumane to perform a major operation on a human being without rendering him first insensitive to pain. In addition, $O(B)$ may also be claimed to hold. Clearly, however, $O(A)$ cannot unqualifiedly be asserted to obtain. In general, not only am I not obliged to administer anaesthetics to any person I can lay my hands on, but I am forbidden to do so because of the toxic effects of such a practice. Thus, even if it were explicitly stated that Fred's welfare depends on being operated on as soon as possible and that he is my patient, it does not yet follow that $O(A)$, unless it is definitely the case that I am about to perform the required surgery. It may be obligatory for me to see to it that B is true, yet in case I chose to be heartless enough and instead go to the golf-course, for instance, I am certainly not required to be even more callous and administer anaesthetics to Fred for no useful purpose.

The point I have just made should seem simple enough, yet as I have said, it has been overlooked by some leading philosophers and continues to be overlooked until the present day. As recently, for instance, as 1981, Tomberlin discussed in great detail what is known as the 'contrary-to-duty' paradox which he claims has not yet adequately been dealt with.[6] In fact, however, the solution requires nothing more than the realisation that (α) is not a valid theorem.

Briefly the paradox runs as follows: We assume the truth of these four statements:

1. Smith steals from John.
2. If Smith steals from John it is obligatory that he is punished.
3. It is obligatory that Smith not steal from John.
4. It is obligatory that if Smith does not steal from John he must not be punished for stealing from John.

Let P be 'Smith steals from John'
   Q be 'Smith is being punished for stealing from John'.
Symbolising:

   (1') P
   (2') $O(Q/P)$
   (3') $O(\sim P)$
   (4') $O(\sim Q/\sim P)$.

Now (1') and (2') yield $O(Q)$, while if we accept van Fraasen's:

$$(F) \quad O(A/C) \ \& \ O(C) \to O(A)$$

(3') & (4') entail $O(\sim Q)$, thus giving a contradiction. But in fact there is no problem here at all since the expression $O(\sim Q)$ cannot be derived from (3') and (4'). The derivation would require (α) which is equivalent to van Fraasen's (F) which, as we have seen, is not valid. The preceeding two sentences are entirely sufficient to do away with this paradox about which so many thousands of words have been written.

   It is interesting to note that Tomberlin does consider the possibility of rejecting

$$(T) \quad O(A/C) \ \& \ C \to O(A)$$

but rules out that possibility, dismissing it as unfeasible, since without (T) he cannot see how some obviously binding obligations might be arrived at. Without entering into any of the details of his discussion, it should be obvious enough that this kind of approach could never establish conclusively any result. But in fact there is no need to speculate over whether certain vital results could or could not be established without (T) since its validity can be demonstrated at once through our method. All we need is to look at the inductive counterpart of (T), namely at

$$(T^*) \quad E(A/C) \ \& \ C \to E(A)$$

(T^*) is obviously valid since given that C is true $Pr(A/C) = Pr(A)$.

Section 4

Inferring arbitrary permissions from irrelevant obligations

G H von Wright, one of the major architects of deontic logic enunciates the following three axioms:[7]

   $B1$ $\sim [O(A/B) \ \& \ O(\sim A/B)]$
   $B2$ $O(A \ \& \ B/C) \leftrightarrow O(A/C) \ \& \ O(B/C)$
   $B3$ $O(A/B \lor C) \leftrightarrow O(A/B) \ \& \ O(A/C)$

To dispel any possible reservations one may have concerning **B3** which may not look as obvious as the first two axioms, von Wright says :[8]

> The following example should convince us of the intuitive plausibility of the third axiom: Suppose we are given the order to see to it that the window is closed should it start raining *or* thunder. Obviously this is equivalent to being given the order to see to it that the window is closed should it start raining *and* see to it that the window is closed, should it start to thunder.

However in a later part of his paper he shows that with sufficient ingenuity an absurdly paradoxical result may be derived from these seemingly innocuous axioms:

> Given that $p \leftrightarrow (p \& q) \lor (p \& \sim q)$ it follows that $O(A/B) \leftrightarrow O[A/(B \& C) \lor (B \& \sim C)]$. But by B3 $O[A/(B \& C) \lor (B \& \sim C)] \leftrightarrow O(A/B \& C) \& O(A/B \& \sim C)$. Consequently, (β) $O(A/B) \rightarrow O(A/B \& C)$.

Hence we have:

(1) $O(\sim A/C) \rightarrow O(\sim A/B \& C)$ Substituting $\sim A/A$, C/B, and B/C in (β).

(2) $\sim O(\sim A/B \& C) \rightarrow \sim O(\sim A/C)$ (1) Contraposition.

(3) $\sim [O(A/B \& C) \& O(\sim A/B \& C)]$ Substituting $B \& C/B$ in **B1**.

(4) $O(A/B \& C) \supset \sim O(\sim A/B \& C)$.   (3) Defn. of '$\supset$'.

(5) $O(A/B) \rightarrow \sim O(\sim A/B \& C)$. (β) & (4) Hyp. Syll.

(6) $O(A/B) \rightarrow \sim O(\sim A/C)$.   (5) & (2) Hyp. Syll.

But of course we cannot entertain the possibility that (6) might be valid since B and C may denote entirely different, logically unrelated circumstances. If (6) were valid then we should be able to infer arbitrary permissions from irrelevant obligations; it would follow for instance that if it is obligatory to hold a rifle when standing guard at Buckingham Palace, then it is permissible to hold a rifle when conducting a religious service in Westminster Cathedral. Von Wright proposes to solve the difficulty by pointing out that $O(A/B)$ and $O(\sim A/B)$ are not contradictory statements, for logic permits both of them to be true at the same time. Admittedly the two duties cannot simultaneously be carried out, but that means only that we can be in a situation where we have conflicting duties. Such circumstances, he claims, are what may be called a moral predicament, like the predicament which arises when a man promises to do the forbidden as Jephta in the Book of *Judges*. Jephta made a solemn vow (which he was obliged to keep) which in the end turned out to require the sacrifice of his daughter (something he was obliged to refrain from doing). Thus matters are put right by invalidating **B1**.

Von Wright's position, however proves to be untenable for at least two reasons. First his rejection of **B1** appears unreasonable and secondly, which is even worse, the rejection of **B1** is of no help.

Let me begin by elaborating the second objection which is quite decisive on its own. Clearly by invalidating **B1**, von Wright is only able to prevent the derivation of (6) but not that of (β), which is obtained without the use of any of his other axioms except **B3**. It is obvious however that (β) is unacceptable.

First of all it is common knowledge that the epistemic counterpart

$$(\beta^*) \quad E(A/B) \to E(A/B \ \& \ C)$$

is not a valid theorem. The reason is that C may strongly enough disconfirm A and thus whatever support A may receive from B is overridden by the disconfirmation provided by C. Similarly the deontic expression is not valid either. For example suppose:

A: I give the loaf of bread I have in the house to X.
B: X is evidently starving and is asking for bread,

then it is reasonable to maintain the $O(A/B)$. However, suppose also that

C: The loaf of bread I have contains a large amount of arsenic

then it is quite obvious that $\sim O(A/B \ \& \ C)$.

I might point out in passing that in view of what we have already learnt in the context of Simpson's paradox, we need not explain the invalidity of (β^*) by referring to the possibility that C might provide strong disconfirmation for A. We have seen in Chapter Five that there are cases in which C on its own may provide so much support for A as to render a belief in A fully justified yet when combined with B its positive effect is cancelled.

It is clear therefore that we must prevent von Wright's derivation of (β) and this can be achieved only if we assume (**B3**) not to be valid. That this assumption is indeed correct is clearly shown by considering the epistemic counterpart:

$$(B^*3) \quad E(A/B \lor C) \leftrightarrow E(A/B) \ \& \ E(A/C).$$

It will be recalled that in the previous chapter it was definitely shown that from $E(A/B \lor C)$ neither $E(A/B)$ nor $E(A/C)$ may be inferred. This means that (**B*3**) is not a theorem.

It should now suffice to say that because of the isomorphism between the two branches of logic the invalidity of (**B*3**) entails the invalidity of (**B3**). However for the benefit of those who do not yet see why this is so let me add the following: Suppose S is the unique empirical situation such that when S obtains, but not otherwise, then there is a duty to bring about A. Suppose also that $E(S/B \lor C)$ and therefore of course $O(A/B \lor C)$. But because of the failure of (B^*3) we know that $E(S/B \lor C)$ is compatible with the falsity of $E(A/B)$ and the falsity of $E(A/C)$. Inevitably therefore $O(A/B \lor C)$ is compatible with $\sim O(A/B)$ and $\sim O(A/C)$.

Section 5

Conflicting duties and conflicting hypotheses

Returning now to $(B1)$, it seems to me reasonable to maintain, contrary to von Wright, that it is valid. Thus in no case where we are confronted with potentially conflicting duties do we end up with the obligation to do, as well the obligation to refrain from doing, the very same thing; the conflict vanishes since the greater duty overrides the smaller. Axiom $(B1)$ is never violated under such circumstances for it is not the case that $O(A/B)$ and $O(\sim A/B)$ hold concurrently. It is either that $O(A/B)$ remains only, in case A is the stronger duty, or else $O(\sim A/B)$ prevails.

And what about a situation in which the two duties are of comparable magnitude? It seems reasonable to say then that the conflicting duties pull me with equal force in opposite directions and therefore cancel one another with the end result that neither an obligation to do A nor to refrain from doing A imposes itself upon me. Once more $(B1)$ is preserved, since in this case the correct think to say is that $\sim O(A/B)$ and $\sim O(\sim A/B)$.

It is worth noting that recently Brian Chellas has expressed his support for von Wright's position and offered a short argument in its favour. Chellas has pointed out that the possibility of both A and $\sim A$ being concurrently obligatory[9]

> . . . is a main feature of some concepts of obligation, that it is, often this, for example, that give moral dilemmas their poignancy.

There is no disputing the poignancy of moral dilemmas. Many of the greatest works of literature would not exist without them and there is hardly anything more riveting than the spectacle of a man being torn by conflicting obligations as for instance between the demands of the state or of his religion on the one hand and his commitments to his beloved ones or personal ideals on the other. But my admission of the centrality of moral conflicts in the drama of human life does not refute a single word of what I have just said. It is still true that when of two incompatible moral obligations one is known to outweigh the other there is no room even for a moment's hesitation as it is clear which overrides the other, and when they are balanced it is unambiguously decided that neither applies. However it so happens that very frequently it is not clear how to *evaluate* the magnitude of opposing duties and establish their relative weight. These are the cases where there is a moral predicament generating inner struggle and arduous deliberation. It however, in no way affects the validity of (**B1**).

I do not wish to cite any further arguments based on the nature of morality in support of the view that objectively speaking there are no moral dilemmas. The issue has already received a great deal of discussion and the interested reader may consult a very recent paper by Earl Conee for arguments of that kind.[10] Let me state however that my main reason for adopting the present view has been provided by the principle of the analogy between deontic and inductive logics. According to that principle anyone who was uncertain about the status of (**B1**) should consider the status of its counterpart in epistemic logic. Now of course few people would want to deny that

$$(\textbf{B1}^*) \quad \sim [E(A/B) \mathrel{\&} E(\sim A/B)]$$

is a valid principle. Here too of course there are two cases to be distinguished. In the first case the amount of evidence for and against A is different. Suppose for example that A stands for Newton's laws of mechanics and the time is just before the discovery of Nepture which accounted for the apparent discrepancy between the movements of Uranus and the implications of Newton's laws. Let B represent what we have just said as well as the description of all the many phenomena that were so successfully accounted for by Newton's laws. Since by the middle of the nineteenth century there was a great deal of evidence to support Newtonian mechanics it is correct to assert $E(A/B)$. However, B has also a component which says that the observed orbit of Uranus has definitely been different from what had been predicted on the basis of A. This amounts to a falsification of A and thus it may well be said that $E(\sim A/B)$. As we know, however, in the judgement of the scientists of that period it was rational to maintain one's confidence in A even though that for a while no one could come up with anything adequate to disarm the hostile evidence. They ruled that the empirical support for A was so overwhelming as to dwarf the refuting evidence with the end result that $E(A/B)$.

Now a couple of words about situations in which the conflicting degrees of confirmation are of the same magnitude:

Suppose

A: There is life in the solar system beside the earth.
B: There are rings around Saturn.

Astronomers are fully convinced about the truth of B. If B is true then of course $A \supset B$ must be true. By *Modus Ponens* $A \mathrel{\&} (A \supset B)$ implies B. According to the hypothetico-deductive method a hypothesis A is confirmed by a true observation statement B whenever A in conjunction with established auxiliary hypotheses (in this case in conjunction with $(A \supset B)$ logically implies B. Consequently $Cnf(A/B)$ should have to be admitted to hold (where '$Cnf(A/B)$' denotes 'B raises the credibility of A') which is rather disturbing. It might be pointed out that there is a difference between $E(A/B)$ and merely $Cnf(A/B)$. This however is not much help since, if confirmation were conceded, acceptability would inevitably follow since if B confirms A so does any number of other established, and entirely irrelevant, empirical statements.

One way of resisting such a conclusion could be to suggest that we abandon the hypothetico-deductive method. Remarkably enough there is at least one philosopher who has seriously urged us to do so. Clark Glymour uses this argument in order to show that the view dominant for so long as to what constitutes the essence of scientific method, is hopelessly flawed.[11] In fact, however, there is nothing to force upon us any such devastating conclusion. What it is correct to say in the context of the present example is that B qualifies as having the *tendency* to confirm A. But substitute $\sim A$ for A in the two premises and the resulting sentences will be the precise mirror image of the original sentences. For, of course, since B is true, so is also $\sim A \supset B$. Thus $\sim A \& (\sim A \supset B)$ logically implies B and hence for exactly the same reason $Cnf(\sim A/B)$ should also be said to be true. Consequently, whatever degree of confirmation B tended to confer upon A, it tends to confer precisely the same amount of confirmation upon $\sim A$. The two opposite and equal tendencies cancel one another and A receives not the slightest bit of support from B. In Section 3 of Chapter 7 we will look further at confirmation theory and at content-dependent implication.

A very important point that has emerged from this discussion, one that does not seem to have been noticed before, is that 'O' and 'E' are also duplicates of another in having the common feature of variable strength. Of course, in the case of duties, unlike in the case of probabilities and hence in the case of degrees acceptance, no one has yet devised a numerical scale of measurement and thus there is no quantitative study of moral duties. However, the comparative magnitude of different obligations is of great interest and its study is essential.

A corollary of this shared feature is that just as in the context of confirmation we disregard $\sim A$ when support for it is outstripped by support for A so, in the moral context, when the reasons for doing A distinctly outweigh the reasons for not doing it the latter are ignored. We are then left with unequivocal obligation to bring about A. On those occasions when we find equal and opposing tendencies, in both cases we apply the principle of the cancellation of symmetrical opposites and the situation is as if none of the opposing considerations existed.

Thus we have had major testimony as to how truly significant as well as useful is the resemblance between deontic and inductive logic. Some philosophers have drawn attention to certain similarities between deontic and modal logic. But the two exemplifications of kinship are entirely different. Not only is there no compelling explanation why modal logic should be analogous to the logic of obligations, and not only has no one so far suggested for what practical purpose the analogy might be exploited but also upon a closer look the dissimilarities between deontic and modal logic appear to outweigh the similarities between deontic and modal logic. While for example there is no system of modal logic in which $\Box A$ does not entail A, OA is of course compatible with $\sim A$. It is to be noted on the other hand that here again inductive logic mirrors the logic of obligation. A proposition A may be highly probable relative to what we happen to know, in which case $E(A)$ is true, nevertheless A may turn out to be false. Now we have encountered another basic feature which the logic of obligations and the logic of confirmation share with each other, a feature absent in modal logic. A proposition is either necessary or not; necessity, unlike credibility and moral duty does not come in indefinitely many degrees.

Section 6

The inapplicability of the rule of conjunction

We previously concluded that von Wright's axiom (**B3**) is untenable. Conversely we also saw his claim that (**B1**) is untenable to be unwarranted. Incidentally it may be useful to note that von Wright himself regarded (**B1**) to be intuitively valid and it was only when Geach pointed out to him that his three axioms led to the absurd (6) (asserting that if A is obligatory under certain conditions then A is permissible under any other arbitrary condition) that he felt compelled to withdraw (**B1**). Now we realise however it was not necessary to declare (**B1**) to be invalid since (**B3**) has been shown to be unacceptable and without it (6) is underivable.

Now I should like to draw attention to the surprising fact that von Wright's opinion regarding the remaining axiom (**B2**), is not right either. Even if we are reluctant to conclude that (**B2**) is definitely false we must admit that it is involved in a so far unresolved difficulty.

The reader may well be wondering how this might be possible: surely to assert that the duty to do A as well as the duty to do B, is no more and no less than the duty to do both A and B, is merely to assert a truism! Furthermore, is anyone known to have denied or even merely queried the validity of (**B2**)? The answer to the last question is that I know of no one who has voiced any objection to (**B2**) and in fact I know of quite a number of philosophers who have explicitly declared the validity of ($B2$). I have also found that other experts in the field like von Kutschera, Hans Lenk, David Lewis, Bengt Hensson and Aziza al-Hibri have approved of it.

The answer to the first question is that admittedly ($B2$) looks as if it were trivially true yet a brief glimpse at the situation in epistemic logic is bound to convince us otherwise. Consider

$$(\boldsymbol{B^*2}) \quad E(A/C) \ \& \ E(B/C) \to E(A \ \& \ B/C).$$

As is known the joint probability of A and B is less than that of A or B alone, in all those cases where each is less than 1 and neither entails the other. In consequence of this, the probability of A as well as that of B may be equal to, or more than, n while that of $A \ \& \ B$ may be less than n. In that case however we would have $E(A/C) \ \& \ E(B/C) \ \& \sim E(A \ \& \ B/C)$. This feature of epistemic logic we have had an opportunity to encounter in the previous chapter where we pointed out that contrary to superficial appearances $[Rp \ \& \ Rq \ \& \ \vdash(p \ \& \ q \supset r)] \to Rr$ is not a theorem. S R Levy has recently stated :[12]

... rational belief in each of a series of propositions does not necessarily carry over into a rational belief in the conjunction of those proportions. ...

It should be clear by now that the invalidity of (B^*2) is bound to render ($B2$) invalid too. For suppose a and b are propositions describing empirical situations and imagine that $a \to OA$ and $b \to OB$. Furthermore let $Pr(a/C) > n$ as well as $Pr(b/C) > n$ while $Pr(a \ \& \ b/C) < n$. In this case then it is rational to believe in each one of a and b but not in the conjunction of those propositions. In our terminology

$$E(a/C) \ \& \ E(b/C) \ \& \sim E(a \ \& \ b/C).$$

Now given that $a \to OA$ and $b \to OB$ it may be said to follow that $E(a/C) \to O(A/C)$ and $E(b/C) \to O(B/C)$. It is also true of course that $E(a \ \& \ b/C) \to O(A \ \& \ B/C)$, but as we have seen we do not have $E(a \ \& \ b/C)$. Thus we do not have $O(A \ \& \ B/c)$ either!

Section 7

The unreliability of intuition

As is well known the common practice of philosophers wishing to compile a list of theorems in the logic of obligations has been to advance any statement that looked intuitively valid and against which there did not seem to be an obvious counter-example. Although nobody could believe that any theorem suggested in this manner has actually been *proven* to be valid, most philosophers could not think of a better way of establishing the soundness of a given theorem-like statement. Naturally, hazards are inherent in the method of assessing the soundness of putative theorems by their intuitive appeal, some of which have come already to our attention. Inevitably, different philosophers will judge the reasonableness of expressions differently resulting in a bewildering number of conflicting axiomatic systems that have been advanced. Numerous propositions have wrongly been assumed to express valid axioms and we have already seen some of the puzzles and paradoxes arising out of this.

I should like to begin this section with one more example which may illustrate more dramatically than any of our earlier examples how misleading a guide intuition may be in the construction of a set of axioms for deontic logic. It involves an expression whose validity strikes one as almost unquestionable. However, if our principle is applied to it, the indication is that the expression is invalid and on further probing it becomes certain that it is not a valid theorem. The expression is listed among von Kutschera's axioms of deontic logic

$$\sim O(\sim B/A) \supset [O(C/A) \,\&\, B) \equiv O(B \supset C/A)].^{13}$$

A variety of ways suggest themselves in which one may argue in favour of von Kutschera's expression. First of all we may remind ourselves of the elementary law of logic called the Law of Exportation which says:

$$(A \,\&\, B) \supset C \equiv A \supset (B \supset C)$$

which seems to imply that in general $O(C/A \,\&\, B) \equiv O(B \supset C/A)$. Now of course in the special case where $O(\sim B/A)$, the truth of $O(B \supset C/A)$ simply follows from the obligation to see to it that B is false which automatically results in the obligation to see to it that $B \supset C$ is true. In that case it need not be also the case that given the truth of both A and B it is one's duty to see to it that C is true. Given however $\sim O(\sim B/A)$ the equivalence follows and this is what von Kutschera's expression tells us.

In addition one may employ one of the many concrete examples to illustrate the propriety of von Kutschera's expression. Take for instance

A: My patient suffers from disease D.
B: I administer my patient drug x.
C: I give my patient large doses of drug y to counteract the harmful side effects of x.

Clearly in the special case in which I am prohibited from administering y to my patient when he suffers from D, i.e. in the special case where $O(\sim B/A)$, $O(B \supset C/A)$ may be true only because I am obliged to see to it that $\sim B$, and that logically implies $B \supset C$. Given however that $\sim O(\sim B/A)$ the equivalence $O(C/A \ \& \ B) \equiv O(B \supset C/A)$ seems to hold.

Let us however now test von Kutschera's expression more rigorously and proceed to determine its status with the aid of our principle based on the strict similarity between deontic and epistemic logic. As we shall recall, in the previous chapter among the counterintuitive results of probability theory we have cited the rather surprising fact that

$$\sim E(\sim B/A) \supset [E(C/A \ \& \ B) \equiv E(B \supset C/A)]$$

is definitely not a valid theorem of epistemic logic. It follows therefore from our principle that its deontic parallel, namely von Kutschera's axiom, cannot be valid either!

It is natural that once we have been assured that a statement does not represent a valid theorem we shall not find it too difficult to construct a counterexample even if earlier we were convinced that none such existed. In general such counterexamples will present themselves in situations where neither B nor C represent a useful state of affairs but where it is important that the material implication between B and C should obtain. To offer a concrete illustration, take

C: Event e takes place at time t.

Suppose that I am an army instructor preparing my charges for the various emergencies they may confront in the battlefield. Suppose also that in a given situation which arises in the course of combat only, it is indispensible for their survival that e should take place as soon as possible. Given that I am responsible for teaching the trainees all the survival tactics they are likely to need, it is imperative that I show them how to ensure that e happens at the time of their need. We assume that it is impossible to make C come true barehanded but with the aid of a mechanism M only, which when put together may be set in action by a simple operation B and that will guarantee that C becomes true. In other words, assembling the mechanism M ensures the truth of $B \supset C$, providing the soldiers the means through which C is brought about upon performing an act that makes B true.

Clearly then, given that

C^*: Event e takes place at t^*

where t^* is some time during the period set aside for the members of my platoon to acquire all the techniques that are likely to increase their chances of survival in battle, then I am duty bound to demonstrate to them during that period how to put together mechanism M. That is, I am obliged to build a contraption which will ensure that $B^* \supset C^*$ is true. If we let A denote the story concerning myself and my trainees we have just told, then clearly

$$O(\sim B^*/A) \text{ and also } \sim O(C^*/B^* \& A)$$

since C^* as such is of no use to the soldier under their current circumstances. Nevertheless $O(B^* \supset C^*/A)$ is true, for I am obliged to assemble now in front of them the apparatus on which their lives may eventually depend, that is, I am obliged to see to it that $B^* \supset C^*$ becomes true. This amounts to saying of course, that von Kutschera's

$$O(\sim B^*/C) \supset [O(C/A \& B) \equiv O(B^* \supset C^*/A)]$$

is false.

Section 8

How to compile a list of valid theorems

From what we have seen so far it is fairly evident that all attempts to develop a system of deontic logic that are guided by intuition alone are bound to fail. They are likely to lead to the adoption of indefinitely many wrong theorems resulting in paradoxes and difficulties which will prevent any real progress. On the other hand once we realise the crucial significance of the isomorphism we have highlighted in this chapter there remain absolutely no obstacles for determining quickly which expression is and which is not a genuine theorem and shall avoid any one of the kind of difficulties encountered before.

By now it should be rather obvious how we should proceed toward such an end. We are to begin by compiling a list of theorems concerning rationally justified beliefs based on probability theory. Then we simply translate each item on that list into its deontic counterpart. The following list contains some theorems of epistemic logic:

$$\begin{array}{ll}
\text{(I*)} & E(A \& B/C) \to (E(A/C) \& E(B/C)) \\
\text{(II*)} & [E(A \lor B/C) \& E(\sim A/C)] \to E(B/C) \\
\text{(III*)} & \sim [E(A/C) \& E(\sim A/C)] \\
\text{(IV*)} & [E(A/B \lor C) \& E(A/\sim B \lor C)] \to E(A/C) \\
\text{(V*)} & [E(A/B) \& E(A/C)] \to E(A/B \lor C) \\
\text{(VI*)} & E(A/B \& C) \to E(A \lor \sim B/C) \\
\text{(VII*)} & E(A/B \lor C) \to [\sim B \to E(A/C)] \\
\text{(VIII*)} & E(A \& B/C) \to E(A/B \& C).
\end{array}$$

By applying our fundamental rule based on the analogy between deontic and inductive logics we at once obtain from the above:

(I) $O(A \& B/C) \rightarrow (O(A/C) \& O(B/C))$
(II) $[O(A \vee B/C) \& O(\sim A/C)] \rightarrow O(B/C)$
(III) $\sim [O(A/C) \& O(\sim A/C)]$
(IV) $[O(A/B \vee C) \& O(A/\sim B \vee C)] \rightarrow O(A/C)$
(V) $[O(A/B) \& O(B/C)] \rightarrow O(A/B \vee C)$
(VI) $O(A/B \& C) \rightarrow O(A \vee \sim B/C)$
(VII) $O(A/B \vee C) \rightarrow (\sim B \rightarrow O(A/C))$
(VIII) $O(A \& B/C) \rightarrow O(A/B \& C)$.

Before examining in detail some of the theorems on our list let me comment briefly on the crucial methodological rule we have kept using here over and over again. It seems to me that even if we were not able to produce an explanation why this rule is valid, the mere fact that it has been found effective in all its numerous applications and that not a single instance is known to occur in which it produces an incorrect result, should be sufficient to ensure its utmost impotance. It so happens however, that there is an elementary principle which clearly guarantees fully the correctness of the rule bridging the two logics. The principle asserts that if S_A denotes a set of empirical conditions obtaining at a given time, conditions which may include a large number of features of my surroundings, my own personal characteristics and state of mind, at which a certain obligation A is said to hold, then at any other time at which S_A should obtain, precisely the same obligation expressed by A will arise. The validity of this principle is entirely independent of any particular moral theory one happens to subscribe to. It is hard to imagine anyone finding it possible to explain how in completely identical state of affairs, sometimes I may have and sometimes I may not have, a specific moral duty. We assume therefore that there is a one-to-one correspondence between particular obligations and certain empirical situations.

Suppose therefore, for example, that S_A and S_B denote the totality of the empirical circumstances under which I am obliged to see to it that A and B are true, respectively. According to (I*)

$$E(S_A \& S_B/S_C) \rightarrow [E(S_A/S_C) \& E(S_B/S_C)]$$

and this we can see now to imply:

$$O(A \& B/C) \rightarrow [O(A/C) \& O(B/C)].$$

Clearly then (I) may be inferred from (I*) and similarly for all the rest.

Let us now have a closer look at (VIII) which may seem less obviously true than perhaps any of the earlier theorems. A number of philosophers subscribe to (VIII) among them Bengt Hensson and Aziza al-Hibri.[14] The latter explains that (VIII) is highly intuitive since it allows for the possibility that a complex obligation be satisfied in stages, without altering that complex obligation at any stage. We of course have arrived at (VIII) simply because we found it to be a counterpart of (VIII*). Should we be called upon to do so we could offer a conclusive justification of the latter in this way:

By the Conjunctive Axiom of Probability
$Pr(A \ \& \ B/C) = Pr(B/C) \cdot Pr(A/B \ \& \ C)$
and of course $Pr(B/C) \leqslant 1$
hence $Pr(A \ \& \ B/C) \leqslant Pr(A/B \ \& \ C)$.

Thus given that $E(A \ \& \ B/C)$ which means that $Pr(A \ \& \ B/C) \geqslant n$ it inevitably follows that $Pr(A/B \ \& \ C) \geqslant n$ and hence $E(A/B \ \& \ C)$.

Now of course our important rule based on the close analogy between the two logics can, as we have seen before, be used for the opposite purpose, namely, to determine that certain expressions that might plausibly be taken to represent theorems of deontic logic do not represent valid theorems. Let me cite here two more examples of such expressions. Bengt Hensson in his important survey article advances

$$(\phi) \quad (O(A/C) \ \& \ \sim O(\sim B/C)) \rightarrow O(A/B \ \& \ C)$$

as an acceptable theorem on which he comments by saying:[15]

An obligation remains an obligation if one does something permitted.

Now (ϕ) and Hensson's brief defence might look plausible to some, but anyone aware of the central role of our methodological principle will not decide the matter before examining the inductive counterpart:

$$(\phi^*) \quad E(A/C) \ \& \ \sim E(\sim B/C) \rightarrow E(A/B \ \& \ C).$$

This formula however would be rejected by all inductive logicians. If for example C stood for the law of gravity and the law ascribing fragility to glass objects and A denoted 'the glass bottle I throw out of the window of my 5th floor apartment is going to break', then it is rational to contend that $E(A/C)$. Let us also suppose that

$B:$ The pavement beneath my window is covered with thick cushions.

Clearly $\sim E(\sim B/C)$ since no law of physics is relevant at all to the question whether or not there are cushions beneath my window. Given B, then the discarded bottle is going to land on a soft surface and is unlikely to shatter. Hence $E(A/B \ \& \ C)$ is false. The invalidity of (ϕ^*) must of course alert us to the fact that (ϕ) is not valid either. After some search for a suitable example illustrating this, the invalidity of (ϕ) becomes indeed fully evident.

Suppose we take

C: Jones was robbed a little while ago.

A: Fred, Jones' neighbour goes to the assistance of the latter.

It is reasonable to assert that $O(A/C)$. Let us suppose that

B: Fred just had a major operation two days ago and finds it very painful even just to sit up in his bed.

Quite obviously $\sim O(\sim B/C)$ since it is by no means forbidden for Fred to have a major operation in the beginning of the week just because his neighbour is robbed in the middle of the week. In fact B may be said not only permissible but even obligatory if it were given that the major operation was the only way to save Fred's life. But no person in Fred's condition can be required to exert himself in order to go to the assistance of anyone. Hence $O(A/B \, \& \, C)$ is false.

I conclude with an example that is similar to one we have discussed earlier in this chapter. Consider:

$$(\psi) \quad [O(A/B) \, \& \, O(B/C)] \to O(A/C).$$

It might well seem that moral obligations are transitive and thus (ψ) is valid. It appears quite plausible that if C generates the duty to bring about B while B itself generates the duty to bring about A then C is bound to give rise, via B, to the obligation to see to it that A is true. However, as is well known the inductive counterpart of (ψ),

$$(\psi^*) \quad [E(A/B) \, \& \, E(B/C)] \to E(A/C)$$

is not valid since the possibility of A given B with certainty may be large enough but not when B is less than certain. Thus we must conclude that (ψ) is not valid either.

Once we become aware of the invalidity of (ψ) it is comparatively easy to find examples showing conclusively that this is so. Take

B: Fred's surgeon performs a major operation on him.

C: Fred is suffering from acute x.

A knowledge of the nature of x may make it obvious that $O(B/C)$. Let us also suppose that

A: Fred's surgeon makes sure that Fred is administered heavy anaesthetics.

Assuming that it is very cruel to operate on a person alive to pain, it is correct to maintain $O(A/B)$. However $O(A/C)$ cannot be asserted since it is highly undesirable to administer heavy anaesthetics to anyone unless he was certain to undergo an operation. It is of course possible for an endless variety of reasons that in spite of Fred's urgent need, his surgeon is not going to perform the required operations. The surgeon may have broken his arm or was detained by the authorities as a suspected drug dealer or because Fred at the moment has a very high temperature. For whatever reason B turns out not to be the case, clearly not only does it follow that the consequent of (ψ) is false but that positively it is obligatory to make sure that $\sim A$.

Section 9

Disjunctive permissions

A basically different paradox, the Paradox of Free Choice Permission was raised by von Wright back in 1968, and has remained a subject for discussion until this very day. An admirably clear detailed treatment of the paradox has been published by Erik Stenius as recently as 1982.[16] The paradox is based on a principle of deontic logic which virtually all accept as valid, namely

$$(\gamma_1) \quad A \to C \text{ implies } O(A) \to O(C)$$

which of course entails that (γ_2) $O(A) \to O(A \vee B)$.

Now von Wright maintains that it follows from the meaning of the expression 'it is permitted that', abbreviated as P, that

$$(\gamma_3) \quad P(A \vee B) \to P(A) \& P(B).$$

As an illustration of (γ_3) we may consider the case of a sign which says 'Residents are permitted to keep cats or dogs' which would be correctly interpreted to mean that residents are permitted to have cats as well as being permitted to have dogs. Then again we have the basic theorem which follows from the definition of O and P:

$$(\gamma_4) \quad O(A) \to P(A)$$

substituting $A \vee B$ for A in (γ_4)::

$$(\gamma_5) \quad O(A \vee B) \to P(A \vee B)$$

(γ_5) together with (γ_3) yield by Hypothetical Syllogism:

$$(\gamma_6) \quad O(A \vee B) \to P(A) \& P(B).$$

But (γ_2) and (γ_6) imply by Hypothetical Syllogism:

$$O(A) \to (P(A) \& P(B)), \text{ hence } O(A) \to P(B)$$

which would, if accepted, be utterly destructive since permission for doing anything whatever, could be derived from a single obligation.

Upon applying our method, however, this paradox vanishes too, since then it becomes apparent at once that (γ_3) cannot be a valid theorem of deontic logic. As we know (γ_3) is equivalent to

$$\sim O[\sim(A \vee B)] \rightarrow \sim O(\sim A) \ \& \ \sim O(\sim B)$$

i.e. $\sim O[\sim(A \vee B)] \rightarrow \sim [O(\sim A) \vee O(\sim B)]$ (by De Morgan),
i.e. $(\gamma_7) [O(\sim A) \vee O(\sim B)] \rightarrow O[\sim(A \vee B)]$ (Contraposition).
The epistemic counterpart of the last expression is

$$(\gamma_7{}^*) \quad [E(\sim A) \vee E(\sim B)] \rightarrow E[\sim(A \vee B)].$$

From the definition of the notion of 'warrantedness' given earlier it follows that

$$E(\sim A) \text{ iff } Pr(A) \leqslant 1-n$$

$$E(\sim B) \text{ iff } Pr(B) \leqslant 1-n$$

and $E(\sim(A \vee B))$ iff $Pr(A \vee B) \leqslant 1-n$, i.e.

$$Pr(A) + Pr(B) - Pr(A \ \& \ B) \leqslant 1-n.$$

Now since $Pr(A \ \& \ B)$ can be as small as zero, it does not follow from $Pr(A) \leqslant 1-n$ and $Pr(B) \leqslant 1-n$ that $Pr(A) + Pr(B) - Pr(A \ \& \ B) \leqslant 1-n$. Thus $(\gamma_7{}^*)$ is invalid and by our principle so inevitably is (γ_7) as well as its logical equivalent (γ_3). Thus just as $A \vee B$ does not entail $A \ \& \ B$, $P(A \vee B)$ does not entail $P(A) \ \& \ P(B)$.

Section 10

Disjunctive obligations and disjunctive hypotheses

The foregoing does, however, not constitute a solution to another paradox due to A Ross which makes no use of (γ_3) and goes as follows:
    Suppose that

    A: I feed the poor.
    B: I comment on the weather to the poor.

Assuming that $O(A)$ obtained, it follows that $O(A \vee B)$ obtains too. But the latter reads, 'It is obligatory for me to see to it that the statement "either I feed the poor or comment on the weather to the poor" is true.' But that statement I can render true by merely commenting on the weather. And no one would agree that by doing so I was discharging any moral duties or accomplishing anything of value.

The solution to this paradox is somewhat more complicated than in the previous case, but we shall see that here too everything becomes completely clear when we look at the inductive counterpart of the theorem underlying the paradox. That $A \rightarrow C$ implies $E(A) \rightarrow E(C)$ is of course a theorem of epistemic logic. Let us suppose that

A :   it is safe to touch the door knob
C :   it is safe to touch the snake lying in the basket in front of me.

Given that the door knob in question is a standard door knob, millions of which are being touched by millions of people every day, the probability of A may be said to be exceedingly high and hence A may be regarded as very firmly established. On the other hand, imagine that the snake referred to by C looks most menacing and like a steel trap ready to spring into lightning action and is known to contain sufficient venom to kill a whole herd of buffaloes. Regardless of this $A \lor C$ is true.

The most important implication of the acceptability of any hypothesis is that it is rational to act upon it. A vital point to make here is one that is by no means always born in mind, that just because it is rational to act upon a given hypothesis, it does not follow that it is rational to act so entirely without qualifications. So it may be rational to act upon a given hypothesis, yet it is not immaterial *how* one acts upon it ; depending on our background knowledge it may be rational to act in one way but not in any other of the ways which also presuppose the truth of the same hypothesis. Clearly it is possible to act in three different ways each of which presupposes the credibility of a statement of the form $A \lor C$: (1) in a way to which only the truth of A but not of C is relevant, (2) in a way to which only the truth of C is relevant, (3) in a way to which the truth of both is relevant. In the example just cited, the acceptability of $A \lor C$ renders it reasonable that I act in the first way and in neither of the other two. My knowledge of the acceptability of $A \lor C$ when combined with my knowledge concerning the nature of the snakes in the basket forbids me to act either in way (2) or (3). Thus our first step must be the appreciation of an important feature of epistemic logic that is by no means widely appreciated: we must distinguish between two separate questions that are to be asked concerning a hypothesis. One is the question whether its credibility has adequately been established, and the second is, supposing the hypothesis to be acceptable, which of the variety of ways in which it is possible to act upon it does reason sanctify?

It may be of interest to note that there are many instances in which a hypothesis is maximally acceptable and yet there is not a single way in which it is rational to act on it. Consider

 P : the most venomous African snake lays eggs, the yolk of which cures
any variety of the common cold.

Let us imagine that I have no sufficient information upon which to decide
the status of *P*, or in other words, neither *P* nor ~ *P* is rationally acceptable
for me. The probability of *P* ∨ ~*P* is, of course, 1, and therefore the
acceptability of *P* ∨ ~ *P* is of the highest degree. In this case acting upon *P*
could consist in my seeing to it that in spite of the vicious nature of the
reptiles in question, they should be allowed to thrive and multiply for the
great benefit of the millions of people suffering from the common cold every
year. But given the lack of adequate evidence to support *P*, it would be
foolish for me to go out of my way and try to promote the welfare of the
species in question. Acting upon ~ *P*, on the other hand, might consist, let
us suppose, in my killing any member of this species on sight. Since I have
no sufficient evidence for ~ *P* either, I should not destroy any such snake
unless I am in danger. It goes without saying that I cannot act in the third
way and perform simultaneously contrary actions. What may be reasonable for me to do is to refrain from all positive action relative to *P* and
~ *P* and avoid having anything to do with those snakes.

The situation in deontic logic faithfully reflects the situation in epistemic
logic. Given *O*(*A*) we may indeed derive *O*(*A* ∨ *B*). But once again we must
distinguish between two separate questions one may ask concerning a
deontic expression: the first question is, does that expression convey an
obligation and the second question is, supposing that it does, which of the
variety of ways in which it is possible to bring about the fulfillment of that
obligation does reason sanctify? In the light of our knowledge that moral
value attaches to *A* but none to *B*, the answer to the last question must be
that the second of the possible ways to act is inappropriate in the context
given. I do not think that there would be many people who, after some
reflection, would insist that there is any genuine difficulty in the inductive
example we have described. A brief reflection should convince one that in
the less familiar deontic context the situation is precisely the same, and no
real problem is left there either.

It is interesting to note that von Wright in a recent article raises the
question whether *FA* → *F*(*A* & *B*) (*F* for 'it is forbidden that') should be
considered a law of deontic logic. He says :[17]

> I do not think that there is any clearcut answer Yes or No to the question. . . .
> Maybe the lawgiver would permit actions of the kind *A* & *B* if they could be done
> (perhaps possessing the characteristic *B* would 'make good' the bad which actions
> with the characteristic *A* have and which motivated the prohibition *FA*).

What is remarkable about this passage is that it shows von Wright having the impression that he is posing a novel kind of problem when in truth his question has been settled immediately with the dissolution of Ross's paradox. After all $FA \rightarrow F(A \ \& \ B)$ amounts to $O(\sim A) \rightarrow O[\sim(A \ \& \ B)]$ which of course is equivalent to $O(\sim A) \rightarrow O(\sim A \ \lor \ \sim B)$. The last expression is precisely the one that worried Ross, and we know that it represents a theorem. However, the question, how one is to make sure that $(\sim A \ \lor \ \sim B)$ is true, will have to be decided according to the context as determined by our background knowledge.

It should appear clear by now that while von Wright makes a valuable point, he has not got matters quite straight. He is right that 'there is no clear cut answer Yes or No' but not to the question he had in mind. Von Wright believed that the question lacking a definite answer is whether $FA \rightarrow F(A \ \& \ B)$ is or is not a law of deontic logic. But the answer is decidedly, *Yes*. It is only to the next question, namely, which one of the ways to ensure that $\sim(A \ \& \ B)$ is true are we to choose, that a context-independent answer cannot be given.

Section 11

The ubiquity of disjunctive statements

It is essential to realise that what we have said concerning the acceptability of disjunctive statements, and the status of disjunctive obligation is of universal relevance since every statement may be represented in a disjunctive form. It is true for every statement A that

$$A \leftrightarrow (A \ \& \ B) \ \lor \ (A \ \& \ \sim B)$$

where B may be any statement. In many cases in which it is impossible to act upon A in any other way than either by presupposing the truth of B or the truth of $\sim B$, it may make no difference in which way I act. However, should it also be the case that I know B alone to be acceptable, then reason required that I refrain from acting in a manner that presupposes the truth of $\sim B$.

For an illustration we may look once more at P, the hypothesis mentioned in the last section, according to which the yolk of a certain kind of egg (Y) cures any variety of the common cold. We shall consider the situation in which P has as a matter of fact been firmly established as a credible hypothesis. Suppose we are confronted with a highly feverish victim of influenza then since $E(P)$, we are certainly rationally entitled to wish to see to it that the requisite amount of Y be introduced into his system. This of course may be accomplished in different ways: the simplest is to make the patient swallow Y. Alternatively we could administer Y

intravenously. We shall remind ourselves that

$$E(P) \leftrightarrow E[(P \ \& \ Q) \lor (P \ \& \ \sim Q)]$$

where we might have

Q: Y causes severe damage to the human digestive system.

Additional information is required in order to determine whether the disjunctive equivalent of P is to be taken as true because of the truth of the first or of the second disjunct, and we shall act accordingly. Clearly, should it be the case that Q has been demonstrated to be highly credible then we shall not be prepared to administer Y orally so as not to damage the invalid further. If the opposite should be true, namely, that $\sim Q$ has been strongly confirmed, then there is no reason why anyone afflicted with the common cold should be subjected to any treatment more strenuous than being asked to swallow Y.

Similar remarks apply to the deontic case as well. For example, suppose that we have

A: I feed the poor.
B: I use my own, and not somebody else's money, to buy food,

then we may assert $O(A)$ and hence its equivalence $O[(A \ \& \ B) \lor (A \ \& \ \sim B)]$. However, since I know independently that it is forbidden to use somebody else's money without their consent no matter how noble the purpose may be, that is, I know that $O(B)$, it follows that the only way in which I am supposed to bring about the truth of it is by acting in a way which presupposes the appropriateness of rendering $A \ \& \ B$ true but not which renders $A \ \& \ \sim B$ true.

Von Wright touches upon this issue as well when he declares that $O(A \ \& \ B) \rightarrow OA \ \& \ OB$ cannot be a truth of logic:[18]

> From the fact that he has been ordered to enter a garden through a certain gate, it does not follow that he ought to enter the garden regardless of how he does it ... if he finds the gate locked and cannot open it then he cannot conclude 'logically' that because of the order given he must now jump the fence—a feat which let us assume he could perform.

In this case A represents 'he enters the garden' and B stands for 'he uses the gate'. It should be obvious by now that since A is equivalent to $(A \ \& \ B) \lor (A \ \& \ \sim B)$, then that statement can be made true either by seeing to it that the first or that the second disjunct is true. But when the subject begins to contemplate in what way he should in fact see to it that the statement is true, then since the obligation to make B true has been asserted, he knows that he is not supposed to make A & $\sim B$ true. Once again therefore von Wright ought not to have said that $O(A$ & $B) \rightarrow OA$ & OB is not a truth of logic; rather, it is. Given that $O(A$ & $B)$ the statement definitely follows, however, it also follows that A must be made true through ensuring the truth of the first disjunct of the complex statement to which A is equivalent, and not of the other disjunct.

Section 12

The refutation of the thesis of partial isomorphism

Ever since Chisholm's important paper in which he compared moral obligations to empirical hypotheses with respect to defeasibility, philosophers have been aware that some degree of similarity existed between deontic and inductive logic. At the same time it has hitherto been taken for granted that the resemblance is partial only. Indeed, there seem to be different examples which suggest with different degrees of plausibility that the isomorphism between these two brands of applied logic is by no means complete. Let us consider two examples that appear to show with different degrees of *prima facie* validity, that there are important dissimilarities between these two disciplines.

(1)   T R Girill claims that there is a structural disanalogy between inductive and deontic defeat.[19] In the former case we have a stronger kind of defeat, one that may be called an 'overriding' defeat, whereas in the latter case we have merely a cancellation. He illustrates his point with the following example:

Take

p: Reliable Ralph said that Ba
q: $(\exists x)Bx$
s: $(x) \sim Bx$.

We have here $E(q/p)$ since Ralph's reassurance may be taken for strong evidence that q, however, when s is added to p, this does not merely cancel the acceptability of q but goes further to render acceptable its denial. In other words, not merely $\sim E(q/p$ & $s)$ but $E(\sim q/p$ & $s)$ is the case.
    On the other hand, take

p: H promises to give his (live) goldfish to K.
q: H gives a goldfish to K.
s: The goldfish dies or K dies.

In parallel to the inductive situation $O(q/p)$ may be said to hold, but the addition of the defeater s does no more than cancel the obligation, it certainly does not make it obligatory that $\sim q$. In other words only $\sim O(q/p$ & $s)$ is the case, but not $O(\sim q/p$ & $s)$.

The flaw with this argument seems to be transparent enough and it is not too difficult to see why one cannot legitimately conclude that the isomorphism between deontic and inductive logic is any less than perfect. Not that there is anything wrong with the particular examples provided by Girill, but why need we conclude on the basis of a single example that in all instances in inductive logic defeat is of an overriding kind and why must we conclude on the basis of another single example that in all cases of deontic logic without exception, the defeat is of the weaker kind? If we happen to look at different examples we shall see first of all that it is by no means obvious that in inductive logic all defeats are overriding defeats. For example, take

p :   Three people told me they saw Fred last week in New York.
q :   Fred was in New York last week.

It is reasonable to say that $E(q/p)$, because of the testimony of three people, especially when given that Fred visits New York at frequent intervals, and therefore even in the absence of positive testimony there is an even chance that he was last week in New York. Now consider

s :   it has been firmly established that the three people referred to in p are compulsive liars.

I believe everyone will agree that $\sim E(Q/p$ & $s)$ but that there is not justification to go any further and claim $E(\sim q/p$ & $s)$, since there is not a shred of positive evidence that Fred was not in New York last week. In other words, it is correct to maintain that $Pr(q/p$ & $s) = Pr(q)$ which as we said before was $\frac{1}{2}$.

Secondly, there are examples in deontic logic where the defeat is an overriding one. For example, imagine

p :   the X-ray picture I have been sent from the lab seems to show clearly that Fred has a very large abnormal growth in his body.
q :   I operate on Fred.

It is reasonable to maintain that $O(q/p)$. But suppose now that we have

s :   I receive an urgent message from the lab saying that some X-ray pictures have been mixed up and that the picture labelled 'Herb' is in fact Fred's picture, and the latter clearly shows Fred's body to be free of any abnormalities.

No lengthy arguments are required to convince anyone that here we have not merely $\sim O(q/p \ \& \ s)$ but also $O(\sim q/p \ \& \ s)$. Given that there is no reason to believe that Fred is in need of having anything surgically removed from his body, I am not merely absolved from, but are strictly prohibited from, performing what would have to be regarded as an entirely superfluous operation.

(2)   It is easy to see that:

$$(\delta^*)\quad E(A \ \& \ B/C) \rightarrow E(A/B \ \& \ C)$$

is a theorem of inductive logic. One way of demonstrating it is by considering the Conjunctive Axiom of probability theory

$$Pr(A \ \& \ B/C) = Pr(B/C) \cdot Pr(A/B \ \& \ C)$$

which implies that $Pr(A \ \& \ B/C) \leqslant Pr(A/B \ \& \ C)$. But given that $E(A \ \& \ B/C)$ iff $Pr(A \ \& \ B/C) \geqslant n$ the antecedent of (δ^*) implies that $Pr(A \ \& \ B/C) \geqslant n$ and therefore $Pr(A/B \ \& \ C) \geqslant n$. Thus $E(A/B \ \& \ C)$ and (δ^*) is a valid theorem of inductive logic. Thus it follows from our principle that

$$(\delta)\quad O(A \ \& \ B/C) \rightarrow O(A/B \ \& \ C)$$

must be a valid theorem of deontic logic.

There are however, certain examples which may suggest that (δ) is not valid and thus the principle of the total isomorphism between deontic and inductive logic may seem to have exceptions. For instance, we may look at the case where we have

A :   all the defective tyres on my car are replaced
B :   the brakes of my car are in perfect shape
C :   only two of my car's tyres are still in satisfactory condition (and it is given that 98 per cent of cars in such a run-down condition do not have adequate brakes any longer).

In some places the law implies $O(A \ \& \ B/C)$ but not $O(A/B \ \& \ C)$. In other words, the law says that if C is the case, then not only is it my duty to see to it that the brakes are repaired, but since my car is in the workshop already, then for additional safety I am also obliged to make sure that the defective tyres on my car are replaced. However, as long as the brakes are in perfect shape, and thus no immediate danger is facing any one, I am not obliged to sacrifice time and energy to see to it that A becomes true. Thus we seem to have a counter example to (δ).

Some might attempt replying that here we are dealing with legal matters which need not meet the demands of deontic logic. The legislature may have the power of exempting anyone from ensuring A when B and C are given, even if reason requires that $O(A/B \ \& \ C)$.

The point concerning the power of the legal authorities is noteworthy and is one I do not wish to contest. However, it does not seem capable of providing a satisfactory solution to our problem. After all we have just argued that it is reasonable to mandate A & B when given C because it is definitely dangerous to drive a car when neither A nor B is made true and given therefore that at least one of them must be rendered true it is not too burdensome to demand that the other is made true too. However, to ask just for A when B is also given could be deemed unreasonable. Thus we cannot claim that the legislature has enacted an 'unreasonable' law.

To find the right answer we must recall that as has been implied by Girill's example just cited, $O(q/p)$ does not entail $O(q/p$ & $s)$. The common account, as correctly indicated by Girill, is that this follows from the defeasability of moral obligations. The duty to ensure the truth of q is never an absolute one; it varies with our background knowledge. However, there is an alternative, useful way of looking at matters. It may be pointed out that obviously $O(q/p)$ does not imply $O(q'/p)$ where q and q' represent different propositions. Now in Girill's example we may be said to have a case like this:

q: H gives live goldfish to live K
q': H gives dead goldfish to K
       or
       H gives goldfish to dead K.

Given that 'ought' implies 'can' and that with the introduction of s—according to which either the goldfish or K has ceased to be alive—H cannot ensure that q is true then no such obligation may apply to him. It is possible for him however to make q' true. But q' is quite a different proposition from q and there are no premises given from which $O(q'/p)$ could be claimed to follow.

Similarly, in our case, when fully spelled out 'A' may be said to stand for 'All the tyres on my car are replaced when this may be done at a time at which other repairs are also being carried out' while 'A^*' stands for 'All the tyres on my car are replaced even if this *cannot* be done at a time at which . . .'. And of course $O(A$ & $B/C)$ does not imply $O(A^*/B$ & $C)$.

It is essential to realise that what has been called 'the defeasibility of empirical hypotheses' may also be looked upon in precisely the same manner. Suppose for instance that we take

h: All ravens are black.
b_1: Since as far back as memory goes, and until yesterday, all the millions of ravens that had been observed were black.
b_2: Today a large number of truthful witnesses report having sighted a great variety of non-black ravens.

The usual way of telling this story would be to say that while $E(h/b_1)$ it is not the case that h remains acceptable in the context of the enlarged background information b_1 & b_2. However, an alternative version of what has actually taken place, exists as well. We begin by pointing out that even after being given b_2 we could continue to subscribe to h provided we postulated some additional hypothesis $h*$ that fully counteracted the effects of b_2 on h. One such hypothesis might be

$h*$: The large number of witnesses reporting today having sighted many non-black ravens were victims of mass-hallucination.

Thus with the introduction of b_2 we have the option of continuing to treat the empirical data as unchanged and of looking upon the hypothesis, the status of which is to be determined, as different now from what we had before. In other words, while earlier we had to assess the effect of b_1 on h now we have to determine the effect of b_1 on h & $h*$. In view of the fact that $h*$ is quite blatantly ad hoc it would be regarded with considerable scepticism unless some strong evidence came to light to lend it specific support. Of course $E(h/b_1)$ does not entail $E(h$ & $h*/b)$ and under the circumstances we should agree that $E(h/b_1)$ while denying that $E(h$ & $h*/b_1)$.

It appears then that our examination of the question of the validity of (δ) instead of leading to our affirming that a definite disanalogy exists has helped us discover an additional facet of the close kinship between deontic and inductive logic.

7

Belief and Understanding

Section 1

The truth-condition analysis of understanding

In this chapter I should like to have a brief look at a point that although important, happens to have received very little attention. The point concerns the intimate link between belief and understanding. One of the few philosophers who at least makes a brief reference to this link is C Ginet who writes:[1]

> . . . S cannot be confident (or even believe) that *p* unless he *understands* the proposition that *p*. He need not understand it as fully as it might be understood. He, might, for example, believe that the university owns a cyclotron without understanding very well what a cyclotron is. But he cannot believe what he does not understand at all.

It seems therefore that if *Cap* denotes '*a* assigns high credibility to *p*' and $U_s ap$, '*a* understands to a sufficient degree the meaning of *p*' then

$$Bap = {}_{df} Cap \ \& \ U_s ap.$$

We note that one source of no small difficulty is the vagueness of 'understanding to a sufficient degree'. No doubt, it should require a considerable amount of work before we would be in general be able to determine precisely how much understanding counts as sufficient for our purposes. Let us look at something that may perhaps be somewhat less strenuous, namely, at the way we might elucidate merely the notion of 'understanding a proposition (or a sentence)' and 'partially understanding a proposition'.

For the purposes of our discussion I shall adopt the view that is held by many contemporary philosophers, namely, that to understand a statement amounts to being able to recognise the conditions under which that statement is true or false. This is called the truth-condition analysis of understanding and those subscribing to it are committed to the view that the ability to recognise some of the truth-conditions of a sentence provides some understanding of it and the more of these a person recognises the greater his understanding. This seems to be for instance Quine's view who in a very brief statement expressing his support of the truth-condition analysis says :[2]

> ... a man understands a sentence in so far as he knows its truth-conditions.

This surely appears to have the sensible implication that one does not either understand a sentence or fail to understand it but that understanding comes in different degrees. The further a person's ability to recognise relevant truth-conditions the greater his understanding. Now Quine uses the phrase 'in so far as he *knows*' but perhaps he would not insist upon it. In the present context it is impossible to demand knowledge rather than mere ability to name those conditions. After all we have just pointed out that the more detailed definition of '*a* knows that *p*', is along the lines of

$$(\phi) \quad Kap = {}_{df} p \ \& \ (Cap \ \& \ U_s ap) \ \& \ JBap.$$

Clearly if the notion of 'understanding' has to be explicated in terms of the notion of 'knowledge' then our definition is circular.

Section 2

The proper formulation of the conditions for partial understanding

It may appear however that there is compelling argument for concluding that (ϕ), which makes essential use of the concept of 'partial understanding', is not an adequate formal definition of '*a* knows that *p*'. It may appear that it is possible at most to explicate the notion of having a complete understanding of a given sentence, since no one is capable of offering a coherent statement of the conditions required for partial understanding. Let me explain.

Suppose I believed that the sentence 'Howard is a coward' (S_1) was false because Howard was a successful test-pilot for the last five years. It should seem reasonable to hold in such a situation that I have at least a partial understanding of S_1. Yet it is conceivable that in fact my ideas concerning S_1 are entirely off target since I believe that 'coward' stands for 'permanently earthbound'. It would then follow that I took Howard's serving as a test-pilot as falsifying S for entirely wrong reasons, namely, because a test-pilot is bound to leave the ground. Should I also believe that another reason why S_1 is false is because Howard is known to have jumped into the raging sea during a hurricane to rescue several people, I still may be completely in the dark as to the correct meaning of S_1. For I may translate 'coward' as 'never floating either in air or water', and so naturally treat both conditions just described as rendering S_1 false.

Some might attempt to argue perhaps that what is required for understanding is not merely holding a correct belief concerning truth-conditions but the *knowledge* of these conditions. A person of course does not know simply by holding a true belief; he also needs to be justified in that belief. Clearly, given that I believe that Howard's being an aviator makes S_1 false for the wrong reason, it follows that my belief that this constitutes a falsifying condition is unjustified and fails to confer knowledge on me.

Surely, however, this reply will not do since it implies a requirement so stringent as to become useless. According to this it is necessary that I should hold that Smith's doing what he does is a falsifying condition for precisely the reason it is in fact such a condition, namely, because that work requires courage. This involves us in the plain circularity of maintaining that in order to know that it is false that Howard is a coward it is necessary to know that Howard is not a coward.

In an attempt to avoid circularity one might perhaps wish to suggest that something less is required than the knowledge of the full reason why being a test-pilot is relevant to the truth-value of S_1. What may still be necessary is that I should at least know what aspect of the condition is the relevant aspect, which in this case consists in knowing that it is not the fact that one is frequently airborne but rather that one is in danger.

This reply will still not do since it would permit someone who utterly misunderstood S_1 to qualify as having understood it. The following example, though somewhat bizarre, it still good enough to illustrate my point. Let us suppose that some people suffer from recurring bouts of painful hiccups that can be stopped only by totally distracting them. The most effective treatment is to immerse the patient suddenly in a very dangerous situation. Conceivably, I could be labouring under the preposterous misunderstanding of taking S_1 to mean that Howard is not suffering from this kind of affliction and hence regard his choice of the career of a test-pilot to be a condition falsifying S_1. I would argue that evidently in order to obtain relief from his constantly recurring unpleasant condition that Howard secured himself a job which involves him daily in considerable danger. His jumping into the stormy sea will for similar reasons confirm for me that Howard is indeed suffering from bouts of hiccups.

Conceivably one might still believe that the situation could be remedied by requiring yet more specific description of the precise elements in

Howard's circumstances that are responsible for them serving as truth conditions for S_1. We might add to what has already been said that I must be capable of identifying the relevant aspect of the situation as Howard's lack of fear of the danger associated with it. However it turns out that even this would be insufficient to eliminate all scope for misunderstanding. I may believe for instance that Howard is suicidal and in such a morbid state of depression that the prospect of going on living is far more intolerable to him than any form of sudden death. Thus Howard may in fact be very cowardly and his willingness to risk death indicates not the possession of courage but utter despair. Howard has in the last few years been in such deplorable state of mind in which he is terrified of life much more than of death.

It should seem sufficiently evident by now that the only way for excluding all forms of possible error is by spelling out fully that the reason Howard's serving as a test-pilot makes S_1 false is because this is a manifestation of him not being a coward. On the other hand it should be obvious that no such difficulties arise when attempting to formulate the conditions for complete understanding. That is, the problem of assigning the correct conditions for the wrong reasons arises only in the context of partial understanding. Someone who is capable of determining of every condition that prevails or might prevail whether it is relevant to S, and if relevant, whether it would render it false or true, has inevitably a genuine understanding of S. In our case for instance, he would have to be assumed to be holding correctly that if Howard was not in a morbid state of mind, and so on, and still serving as a test-pilot then that would imply that S_1 was false. It seems therefore that while complete understanding may be said to be secured by a perfect ability to recognise all the truth-conditions of a given sentence, partial understanding cannot be defined without circularity.

However, we can overcome our difficulties by changing our approach so as to bypass the kind of problems just described. Let us first look at the following attempt to describe partial understanding:

> A person a understands S at least to some extent if he believes C (which are in fact truth-conditions for S) to be truth-conditions for S, and he does so for the same reasons that all those who fully understand S believe C to be truth-conditions for S.

This definition avoids reference to a's belief in C constituting truth-conditions 'for the right reason' which as we have seen is either insufficient to prevent misunderstanding or involves us in circularity. But of course this definition would still leave us with the task of describing those who may rightly be regarded as understanding S. In other words we have done no more than define 'understanding' in terms of understanding. This however in view of what we have said can be remedied by revising the last phrase to read:

> ... and does so for the same reasons which anyone who was capable of recognising *all* the truth-conditions would believe *C* to be among those conditions.

Section 3

The need for content dependent conditions

Having concluded that partial understanding exists and is capable of definition we can approach the central point of this chapter. It may be true that the ability to recognise some truth-conditions results in some amount of understanding, it is absolutely certain that there is a considerably large set of truth-conditions members of which do not provide the slightest amount of understanding. Consider the following cases:

(I) Suppose that I have never heard the word 'coward' before and hence have no real idea what the sentence

S_1' : The coward living at 109 Elm Street, is Howard

is about. However I happen to know and approve of Russell's theory of descriptions. I may thus be aware that when the term 'the coward living at 109 Elm St.' refers to nothing, as when no human being lives at that address, then S_1' must be false. Thus I may be aware of at least one condition that will make S_1' false, yet it should seem absurd to hold that this piece of knowledge provided me with any clue about S_1''s meaning. To put it differently, a person who had any degree of understanding of S_1' and was ignorant of Russell's theory but later became acquainted with it, his understanding of S_1' would remain precisely the same it was before. Thus the truth-condition in question must for one reason or another be irrelevant.

(II) In general when a person a is capable of recognising the truth-conditions for S, but has a defective understanding of some of these conditions then the right thing to say seems to be that a has some understanding of S. For example, let us suppose that a knows that 'There is a bat in the barn' (S_2) is true if there is a flying mammal in the barn, then a may be said to have a good understanding of S_2. Suppose however that a does not fully grasp the term 'mammal' since instead of believing that a mammal is an animal nourishing its young with milk secreted by its mammary glands a merely believes that it is an animal nourishing its young with some bodily secretion or other. If we agree that a must be said to have some idea what it is to be a mammal, then I believe we must also agree that a cannot be regarded as absolutely ignorant of what S_2 is saying. In general it is reasonable to maintain that to the extent to which a person's understanding falls short from being complete, varies directly with the degree of lack of understanding he suffers from with respect to the truth-conditions of that sentence.

In view of this the following question seems to arise. Consider the sentence

S_1^*:   Howard is a coward or a dullard

and assume that a has a full grasp of 'dullard' but not of 'coward'. I believe it will be agreed that a has a partial understanding of S_1^*. Now we shall also assume that a knows enough logic to appreciate that given S_1^* as well as that Howard is not a dullard, then S_1 (i.e. 'Howard is a coward') follows logically. Nevertheless I am quite sure that no one would be prepared to grant that a's knowledge that these conditions implied the truth of S_1 confers the slightest amount of understanding of S_1. Do we have to conclude that contrary to what we have said, truth-conditions not fully understood provide no understanding whatever? The correct answer seems to me that once more we have hit upon conditions that for some reason are irrelevant.

(III) Once more we consider the situation in which I have never heard the word 'coward' before. I have however a friend Fred who has proven himself to be a most reliably truthful person. I know therefore that if Fred should assert that S_1 was true then S_1 must be true. Once again it would seem absurd to claim that my knowing this contributes in the slightest to my understanding of S_1.

It might appear that the last example could easily be taken care of. I believe most philosophers would be prepared to admit that only necessary but not contingent truth-conditions are capable of producing understanding. For example many people assume nowadays that a great many of our psychological dispositions are influenced by the chemical substances in our bodies. It would therefore not necessarily belong to the realm of pure science fiction to speculate that eventually it may be discovered that the amount of a certain chemical, let us say chemical λ, in the bloodstream determined the amount of courage of a person. Suppose that I have a most ludicrous misconception concerning the meaning of 'coward' taking it to be the medical term for a repressed craving for cookies. I am however a chemist and well acquatined with substance λ. Suppose I read in the standard textbook that any person in whose bloodstream the concentration of λ was way below a certain magnitude is invariably cowardly. I cannot imagine that anyone should wish to suggest that my knowledge that the particular condition of Howard's blood, namely, it being deficient in λ, makes S_1 true, provides me with any amount of understanding. In fact after learning about the correlation in question one can continue to misconstrue the meaning of S_1, even to such a preposterous extent as I have done, just as easily as before.

The obvious answer, perhaps, is that in this example we have been dealing with contingent conditions which do not determine meanings. If the laws of nature were different from what they happen to be and substance λ has no relation to the degree of courage an individual had, S_1 would still continue to mean what it meant before. My awareness of this condition does not therefore provide me with a grip on the meaning of S_1. Consequently, someone could have a full understanding of S_1 without knowing about this particular condition. Suppose, however, that Howard has been a highly successful test-pilot for the last five years. If I should be aware of the correct reason why the presence of this condition renders S_1 false, then I should be regarded as someone who understands S_1. This last condition is analytically linked to the falsity of S_1. It is logically impossible that Howard's serving as a test-pilot under standard circumstances should cease to be relevant to the truth-value of S_1, while S_1 continues to mean exactly what it meant before.

This simple account however will not do in the context of the question: what about my knowledge that if a being, whose essence it was to be omniscient testified to the veracity of S_1 then S_1 must be true? Here the implication seems to be a logical implication and my knowing it does not help me to grasp the meaning of S_1.

It appears to me however, that the correct explanation in the case of all three examples is the same. A very basic point concerning truth-conditions that have the power of providing genuine understanding is that they have an intimate connection with the specific contents of the sentence they are to illuminate. It is only when a given set of conditions constitutes truth-conditions by virtue of the particular statement conveyed by S that the knowledge of these conditions is enlightening. When conditions are such that they ensure the truth or falsity of S quite independent of its content, when we can determine that these truth-conditions without having to know what statement is expressed by S then the conditions in question can contribute nothing to our understanding of S.

Let me try and explain this matter in greater detail and rigour. Whenever q follows from p then the implication (IM) may be one of two kinds, differential and non-differential. If IM is differential then it is content-dependent, for in that case the fact that q follows from p is due to the particular contents of q. When IM is non-differential, then, it may be said to be content-independent. We may now present the following definition:

(D) An implication $p I M q$ is *non-differential* if it is not dependent on the specific denoting terms present within q. If x is a term present within

q (which may itself occur also as a component of p) and if x denotes a particular or a universal, then $pIMq$ is non-differential if it continues to hold whenever any other such term is substituted for x.

Examples illustrating the application of **(D)** should prove helpful. *Example 1* Suppose

p_1 : All ravens are black and i is a raven.
q : i is black.

Here we are presented by $p_1 I M_D q$ where IM_D is easily shown to be content-dependent. It makes a crucial difference what specific predicate occurs in q; if we replace 'black' by some term like 'red', 'round', 'fat', etc. the implication will cease to hold. Similarly, if we substitute for i the name of any other individual then p_1 will no longer imply q.

Thus we have to conclude that IM_D is content-dependent, since it holds only as long as the specific contents denoted in q are given.

Example 2 Take

p_2 : If i weighs more than 2 lb then i is black and i weighs more than 2 lb.
q : i is black.

We note that p_2 may be represented as $(q \supset r) \& q$ which is immediately seen to entail q no matter what q stands for. Thus we have here $p_2 I M_I q$. It is clear enough that the implication holds regardless of whather we change 'black' into any other predicate or i in to any other name (remembering of course that all the changes we introduce into q are to be introduced at all its occurrences and that here q also occurs as the consequent in p_2). We conclude therefore that IM_I is content-independent. q may indeed stand for any sentence whatever without it interfering with the existing implication, which therefore has proven itself not to be a function of the particular contents q happens to have.

The basic distinction just described does not happen to be one we are likely to read about in textbooks on deductive logic. The explanation for this is that IM_I is precisely of the same validity as IM_D and from a formal point of view absolutely nothing distinguishes one kind of implication from the other. However, when what we are trying to establish is not merely the presence or the absence of an implication for its own sake, but whether or not a certain practical objective can be accomplished through the existing implication, then the crucial importance of the difference emerges. We should be able to anticipate at this stage already that IM_D is a more significant relationship, in that it provides a more intimate link between p and q than IM_I. The latter is not rooted in the specific nature of s—the statement conveyed by q—and is unaffected by the fact that q expresses s or

$\sim s$ or some statement entirely irrelevant to s. On the other hand, IM_D is a selective relationship as it is genuinely connected to the unique message conveyed by q.

Section 4

The application of the distinction to confirmation

Before tackling 'understanding' in full detail let me illustrate my point by considering the application of our distinction to the notion of 'confirmation'. Clark Glymour, as we saw in Chapter Six, raises objections to the hypothetico-deductive $(H-D)$ method. The $H-D$ rule of confirmation may be stated as follows:

A true statement O confirms a hypothesis H if,
  (i) H and A entail O, where A is a set of auxiliary hypotheses established to be credible and
  (ii) A on its own does not entail O.

Glymour points out that according to this we would have to agree to the absurdity that every H is confirmed by every statement O since by putting $A = H \supset O$ then the $H-D$ rule is satisfied.[3]

Now it is clear that in Glymour's example H & A implies O non-differentially, since one can determine that O follows from H & A without having any idea what terms O consist of. But a reasonable suggestion is that the $H-D$ rule should be adopted with the proviso that the *only* kind of entailment through which confirmation can be conferred on a hypothesis is the differential kind, where the relation H has to O exists only by virtue of the specific statement expressed by O, that is, it exists only because O corresponds to certain facts that happen to obtain.

It is possible to offer several explanations why non-differential impli-cation is to be regarded insufficient for the purposes of confirmation. For example, in order for an hypothesis to be genuinely contingent it is essential that there be some possible worlds in which there exists evidence to support it and also some in which there is none. But if O were implied non-differentially by H & A and if O were permitted to serve as confirming evidence, then H could not be an empirical hypothesis since if O constitutes evidence in the actual world, it constitutes evidence in every possible world no matter what facts happen to obtain, O can be suitably adjusted to correspond to them. That is, since the implication remains unaffected by any changes the terms occurring in O may undergo, we are at liberty shape O in such a way that it will always express a true observation statement.

Another explanation we might offer was anticipated in Chapter Six: suppose it is a fact that a particular a has property ϕ. In that case if a theory implies the statement ϕa, then the latter may be regarded as lending confirmatory support to the theory. At the same time any theory which implies $\sim \phi a$ is of necessity disconfirmed by the same facts. But since O is implied non-differentially, the term $\sim \phi$ may be substituted for ϕ in O, without affecting the implication. Thus H & A (which implies O) would therefore both be confirmed and disconfirmed by O. It is therefore very reasonably ruled to be neither confirmed nor disconfirmed by the proviso requiring differential implication.

In fact, however, most people will find elaborate explanations quite unnecessary. Philosophers may of course differ widely as to what constitutes confirmation of what, but this much is practically self-evident: a sentence O cannot be regarded as confirming anything when we have no idea what observation O describes. Surely the capacity of O to provide support to a hypothesis must be dependent in *some* way on what it says. It is obvious therefore that IM_D is the required relationship in the confirmation of hypotheses.

Section 5

Selective implication and understanding

Returning now to the truth-condition analysis of understanding, the point to bear in mind is that not all truth-conditions are effective in producing understanding, but only those that render S true or false because of the specific statement S in fact conveys. This is obvious enough not to require any elaboration, yet at the same time it would amount to a virtually useless point if nothing more could be added to it. After all, nobody is likely to dispute the claim that I am capable of grasping the characteristic meaning of S only with the aid of something that is uniquely relevant to that meaning. However, the inevitable question arises: how am I to determine whether this is so unless I already know what the specific meaning of S is? In view of what has been said in the previous couple of paragraphs we do not actually face such a difficulty. The crucial feature to be present in truth-conditions C is fortunately one that is easy to discern without having any prior knowledge of S's meaning. All I need to establish is that C implies S differentially, and that of course may be accomplished with the aid of definition (D). As soon as I am assured that the implication is differential one, I may be certain that it is content-dependent, i.e., the implication exists only by virtue of the unique assertion made by S, only by virtue of what S happens to mean specifically.

It should be understandable then why the condition making use of Russell's theory of description is incapable of promoting one's comprehension of S'_1. If the English language changed and the word 'coward' indeed stood for a suppressed craving for some food item, S'_1 would be just as false in the absence of a person answering the description given by that sentence. Consequently it is clear that this particular truth-condition is in no way related to the specific content of S'_1 and hence is not the kind of condition the knowledge of which may provide any help in making S'_1 intelligible.

Consider on the other hand my knowledge that if it is a fact that Howard has been a successful test-pilot for the last five years then this may well be a factor in rendering S'_1 false. In this case I seem to know a condition that genuinely promotes understanding. And indeed this is decidedly a differential condition. In this case the condition mentioned could completely lose its relevance should the word 'coward' change its meaning.

It is quite easy to see now how to account for examples (II) and (III). Supose we replaced the word 'coward' in S^*_1 by ψ where ψ may stand for anything we like. Obviously, 'Howard is not a dullard' together with 'Howard is a dullard or a ψ' entails that 'Howard is a ψ'. Hence the hypothetical syllogism which ensured the truth of 'Howard is a ψ'. Once more then we are dealing here with non-differential and hence useless truth-conditions. Similarly, when an omniscient being assures us that S is true we are confronted by non-differential conditions; we need not know what in particular is being conveyed by S in order to be absolutely certain of its veracity.

Section 6

Further theorems of epistemic logic

On the basis of what we have said so far we may advance as a formal definition of 'a fully understands p':

$$Uap =_{df} (N)(N \leftrightarrow p) \to RaN)$$

where $\leftrightarrow$ is a special symbol denoting content-dependent implication and RaN means 'a recognises N to be one of the truth-conditions for p'. In order to define partial understanding it would not be sufficient merely to change the universal to an existential quantifier in the definition just given. As we have seen in Section Two of this chapter in order to secure partial understanding something more than the bare recognition of the relevant truth-conditions is required. Furthermore even if we succeeded in symbolising adequately the notion of partial understanding that is needed in the present context we would still be a considerable distance from a fully detailed definition of '*a* knows that *p*'. For that we need the notion of *sufficient* partial understanding and we lack even a most rudimentary explication of that concept.

I may mention at this point that in this entire book no reference has been made to a problem that has attracted far more attention in the last twenty years than any other issue in the theory knowledge, namely, the so-called Gettier problem. I do not wish to repeat here the reasons I gave elsewhere why this famous problem is a rather trivial one and was recognised as such by its original proponent Bertrand Russell.[4] The discussion of this chapter alone should be sufficient to convince the reader that there are still interesting, genuine issues on which so far hardly any work has been done at all and that therefore philosophical attention ought to be more evenly distributed over the various significant aspects of epistemology.

In conclusion I should like to point out that there is no need to wonder at this stage about the question raised at the very beginning of the first chapter, namely, whether there are any theorems specific to epistemic logic. Consider for example:

$$(\alpha) \quad (N)[(N \leftrightarrow p) \rightarrow \sim RaN] \rightarrow \sim Kap.$$

This says that if a person is incapable of recognising a single one of the truth-conditions for *p* then (even though *p* is true and he has had the most reliable assurances that regardless of what it is that *p* may be saying it is definitely true) that person does not know that *p*. The reason, of course, is that in a case like this *a* certainly has not got the slightest understanding of the meaning of *p* and therefore his belief amounts to no more than an ultimately contentless conviction that, whatever the string of words constituting *p* mean, *p* must be expressing a true proposition. On the reasonable view advanced by Ginet which we have cited at the beginning of this chapter this is not the kind of belief that is sufficient to confer knowledge.

It is quite probable that expression (α) has never before appeared in print. Nevertheless I am pretty certain that virtually every one who subscribes to the truth-condition analysis of meaning and to the view that belief requires a certain degree of understanding will readily grant that (α) is a theorem of epistemic logic.

It is quite clear that (α) is not strong enough to cover adequately all the cases in which a person is prevented from possessing knowledge because of a lack of an appropriate understanding since even if he is able to recognise some N, and thus have a partial understanding of p, this may not be enough. I do not propose to probe into this matter any further and shall only point out that it may be possible that a stronger theorem

$$(\beta) \quad (\exists N^*)(N^* \leftrightarrow p \ \& \ \sim RaN^*) \rightarrow \sim Kap$$

also holds. $N*$ here means 'a vital truth-condition' and it is being assumed that a small subset of all the truth-conditions may be vital in the sense that if a is unable to recognise any member of this set then he lacks the kind of partial understanding that is sufficient for the acquisition of knowledge.

8

The Verification Theory of Meaning

Section 1

An unheard-of rule of epistemic logic

One of the more far-flung ramifications of elementary, formal epistemic logic touches upon the verification theory of meaning. It involves the simple logical rule known as *Distribution*. As we know, certain operators in epistemic logic obey that rule, others do not. For example $K(A \& B) \rightarrow KA \& KB$ is valid, since the operator K distributes but $M(A \& B) \rightarrow MA \& MB$ is not, since M does not. The reason here is that a conjunction is false as soon as one of its conjuncts is false and thus $M(A \& B)$ may be the case because both A and B are believed, although only A is false and so belief in B is not mistaken.

An interesting question to raise is whether

$$\Diamond K(A \& B) \rightarrow \Diamond KA \& \Diamond KB$$

is true. As we shall find to our surprise in some cases it is and in some cases it is not; the answer essentially depends on what A and B stand for. As we shall see the failure to realise this may have far reaching philosophical consequences. But let us begin at the beginning.

It is common knowledge that verificationism has been left for dead by many. Yet others find it hard to resist the 'perennial attractiveness of verificationism'.[1] Some simply lapse into verificationist talk inadvertently. And there are also some philosophers who have quite recently explicitly championed it. Michael Dummett criticises the view according to which the meaning of a sentence is determined by the truth-conditions that may or may not obtain independently of our capacity to tell if they do or do not obtain. He suggests that instead of truth, as the fundamental notion of a theory of sense, we employ the notion of warranted assertibility or the notion of verification.[2] Also in a recent debate concerning the possibility of absolute frames of reference, between J L Mackie, Jon Dorling and Elie Zahar the question of verifiability plays a central role.[3]

It will be interesting to examine a new type of attack on verificationism, a type of attack which aims at showing *conclusively* that verificationism is untenable. For the first two or three decades in its history, efforts were concentrated on showing that verificationism was implausible. The line adopted by the critics was to find fault with the successive formulations of a criterion of verifiability. After a while, when a great number of these proved deficient, it was claimed that this should be taken as an indication that the whole enterprise had been ill-conceived.

J L Mackie's recent, ingenious attempt to refute verificationism conclusively by showing that its basic assumption leads to a contradiction discusses the following proof, originally advanced by H L A Hart:[4]

(1) $p \,\&\, \sim Kp$ Assumption
                              (That is, we assume that there exists some proposition p which though true is not known. Nobody would insist that we do know every true proposition.)

(2) $\Diamond K(p \,\&\, \sim Kp)$ from (1), by rule R that anything can in principle be known.

(3) $\Diamond(Kp \,\&\, K \sim Kp)$ from (2), distributing K.

(4) $\Diamond(Kp \,\&\, \sim Kp)$ from (3) (since $Kq \to q$).

This, then is a *reductio* proof that something must be wrong with one of the previous steps. But the only plausible candidate is rule R that anything true can in principle be known. In other words, if Q is $p \,\&\, \sim Kp$, then even though Q may be true it cannot be known. It cannot be known to be true because Q cannot be verified to be true. But since Q is true it is obviously meaningful. It follows therefore that Q can be meaningful even though it is in principle unverifiable. Mackie argues, however, that this does not really disprove verificationism, since:[5]

> . . . this way of using the argument refutes only a very strong form of verificationism in which 'verified' entails 'true'; otherwise 'What is verifiable can be known' does not hold.

It seems however that Mackie's defence is of no help at all to verificationism. Let 'Wp' stand for 'p is weakly verified' and let

$$Wp = Pr(p) \geqslant m$$

where m may be quite a small number say $\frac{1}{10}$ or even $\frac{1}{100}$. Then clearly

(1') $p \,\&\, \sim Wp$

is true for some proposition p, since there are obviously true propositions which are not even very weakly verified.

(2') $\Diamond W(p \,\&\, \sim Wp)$

from (1') by Rule R' (to which Mackie agrees) that anything true can, in principle at least, weakly be verified.

(3') $\Diamond (Wp \,\&\, W \sim Wp)$ (from (2'), distributing W).

But now we note that $\sim Wp \to Pr(p) < m$ and hence $W \sim Wp \to Pr[Pr(p) < m)] \geqslant m$. Consequently, from (3'):

(4') $\Diamond (Pr(p) \geqslant m \,\&\, Pr[Pr(p) < m] \geqslant m)$

where of course the first conjunct amounts to $Pr[Pr(p) < m] = 0$, and hence (4') is self-contradictory. Thus we have a *reductio* proof that shows why some true propositions cannot even be very weakly verified. Proof (1')–(4') is of course parallel to (1)–(4), and if there are grounds for believing that strong verificationism has been refuted then there are precisely the same grounds for believing that any sort of verificationism has been refuted.

There is, however, an easy reply to Hart's objection. It is commonly agreed that a sentence is meaningless if it conveys no statement that is either true or false. Thus a sentence that conveys a falsehood is definitely meaningful. But $\sim Q$ (that is, $p \,\&\, \sim Kp$) can be, and has been, verified, and therefore we may continue to tie meaningfulness to verifiability since what is false, no less than what is true, is meaningful. For exactly the same reason Hart's example discussed by Mackie does nothing to discredit verificationism since his expression, when false, can definitely be verified to be so and that is enough to render it meaningful. Here is an easy way to show it:

(1*) $\sim(p \,\&\, \sim Kp)$ Assumption
(2*) $\Diamond K \sim (p \,\&\, \sim Kp)$ from (1*) by R
(3*) $\Diamond K(\sim p \lor Kp)$ from (2*) by De Morgan

and of course (3*) harbours no contradiction.

But what if we assumed that Hart and Mackie hold that according to verificationists, unless a sentence is both verifiable as true and as false it is devoid of meaning? Surprisingly enough even this would be of no help since it turns out that there is a far more radical point to be made. On a closer look it becomes evident that Hart's fascinatingly neat logical exercise, does not in fact lead to any contradiction! Hart, Mackie and Swinburne only thought that it did because they have all overlooked a somewhat subtle error involved in one of the steps in the derivation that led to their conclusion.

One way of making the error clear is by the use of the possible world interpretation of modal expressions. Accordingly, R which says 'Anything true can in principle be known' amounts to 'Anything actually true is in fact known in some possible world (W)'. Consequently we must be mindful of the difference between K_A and K_W which stand for 'it is known in the actual world' and 'it is known in W' respectively.

Clearly then (2) $\Diamond K(p \;\&\; \sim Kp)$ can be rewritten as

(2') $K_W(p \;\&\; \sim K_A p)$

from which we may derive

(3') $K_W p \;\&\; K_W \sim K_A p$

leading to nothing more than the conclusion

(4') $K_W p \;\&\; \sim K_A p.$

Obviously there is no inconsistency in saying that something is known in one world and is not known in another! Hart's conclusion is equivalent to

(4*) $K_W p \;\&\; \sim K_W p$

which of course is self-contradictory but has been arrived at through an illegitimate use of distribution.

This small yet not entirely unimportant point concerning a characteristic aspect of formal epistemic logic does not seem to be generally known since even such eminent philosophers as Hart and Mackie have overlooked it. Their oversight has led them to an erroneous conclusion which can no longer be regarded of small significance.

Thus what we would need in order to construct a viable argument basically along the line of Hart's argument is to consider $Q^* = p \;\&\; \Box \sim Kp$. It would have to admitted that Q^* is *in principle* unverifiable and the only question is, is there any p that would satisfy it? It has been suggested that any number of such p's exist, e.g.:

p_1:   It is raining, but it is logically impossible to verify it.

In my *Aspects of Time* I have objected to this:[6]

... it seems to me that one need not be a logical positivist in order to begin wondering, what sort of a rain are we talking about? It cannot be anything like ordinary rain, which can in principle be seen, heard and felt and whose absence is very strongly confirmed when nothing is seen, heard or felt! It seems evident that in the utterance reference is made to something which we are incapable of describing coherently; that the familiar term 'rain' is not employed at all in a recognisable sense, and thus the sentence has no meaning.

Not everyone will agree. Admittedly p_1 does not refer to a familiar kind of rain. Some will insist however that we can coherently describe a downpour that is such that it is part of its essence to escape human detection. They would also protest that it would be arbitrary to refuse to acknowledge p_1's intelligibility. It is perhaps however superfluous to engage in any argument of this sort since it might be denied that there is compelling reason not to condede the meaninfulness of all sentences like p_1. The verificationist does not necessarily face a problem here. What we have is a sentence of the form

q, and it is in principle unverifiable that q,

where q may of course stand for absolutely anything we like. This obviously means that the source of the unverifiability with which we are presented has nothing to do with the specific contents of p. It is not possible to identify a crucial deficiency in the peculiar facts referred to by p and place the blame on them for the unverifiability of that sentence. It stands to reason that unverifiability may preclude meaningfulness provided it is intrinsically connected with the specific nature of a given sentence; provided it is the purported content of a sentence that stands in the way of verification. The unverifiability of p is a non-differential one and is not effective in depriving it of its putative meaning.

Section 2

Further uses of the vital distinction between the two types of implications

In the previous chapter we introduced the crucial distinction just used between content-dependent and content-independent implication and had the opportunity to see how indispensable the distinction is for the proper understanding of some basic aspects of epistemology. Now I should like to have a brief look at some further very important uses of this distinction. This involves what is probably the most famous attempt to discredit verificationism which, instead of claiming that it disqualifies a great number of meaningful sentences, tries to show that it confers meaningfulness on nonsense. Recall that in the thirties A J Ayer put forward the following suggestion:[7]

A sentence S has empirical significance (or is empirically meaningful) if there are subsidiary hypotheses that, together with the sentence, entail some observation sentence O not entailed by the subsidiary hypotheses alone.

Way back in 1939, of course, Isaiah Berlin complained that Ayer's suggestion is completely useless, since, if accepted, every sentence is meaningful.[8] The reason is very simple. Let S be any sentence whatsoever and O some observation sentence: then, by *Modus Ponens*, S together with $S \supset O$ entails O while the subsidiary hypothesis $S \supset O$ on its own does not entail O. Hence, S must be regarded as meaningful by Ayer's criterion.

Let me invite attention to several remarkable points. First of all, Berlin's objection involves as we shall see a basic misconception. However, this has not inhibited others who have dealt with the topic from regarding his argument as completely devastating. When I say 'others', I include the defenders of verificationism among them. Even Ayer himself was convinced that Berlin's clever argument had destroyed his criterion and went on to construct a more elaborate one immune to that attack. Against this, however, Church raised an even more ingenious objection that was based on exactly the same error as before. Skipping a few decades, we find, as recently as 1980, Clark Glymour's book already discussed citing with full approval Berlin's attack on Ayer's original proposal.[9]

By now it is probably not necessary to explain at great length why the whole debate under review could have been avoided. Anyone who holds that meaningfulness is grounded in verifiability must surely have in mind verifiability that is vouchsafed by the particular contents of a given sentence. In the case of Berlin's example, it is obvious that the connection between S and the observation sentence O is not the wholesome kind that is capable of conferring significance upon the former. It is clear that he has presented us with a typical non-selective, content-independent implication for two reasons: first of all S may stand for any sentence imaginable without it having any effect on $S \supset (S \supset O)$ implying O, and secondly it matters not whether O denotes a given statement or its denial.

Clearly those who are prepared to accept verifiability as a guarantee for meaningfulness do so because they assume that an expression with genuine content must have meaning and that an expression which is instrumental in the yielding of an observation sentence cannot be devoid of content. But when the observation sentence is produced through observation-independent implication, we have in fact no evidence of the presence of any content and therefore no reason for regarding the expression as meaningful.

Thus Ayer needed to say nothing more in replying to Berlin than that in his criterion the term 'entail' is to be understood as 'entail selectively' and that naturally the implication between the sentence S and the sentence O from which it is to derive its significance, has to be content-dependent. It is fascinating to contemplate the difference it would have made to the history of analytical philosophy of the last forty-five years had this small, exceedingly simple but crucial point been made at the time. It is not merely that so many ingenious papers attacking and defending verification would have remained unwritten, but the entire development of our ideas concerning meaning and empirical significance would have taken a different direction.

It may be useful to look additionally at a more recent attempt to refute verificationism. I am not sure who originated this argument but have heard several people claim that they regard it as the best of all the objections that have been made. Suppose there exists a unique person SP, a Super-Predictor, who is capable—without employing any method, but simply saying whatever first comes to his mind—unfailingly to predict the future. Let us assume it as an undisputed fact that in millions and millions of past occasions SP's predictions have turned out to be true and that there have been no occasions on which he was wrong. Now consider

$S:$ The event e has happened

where e is described as an event which has not the slightest effect on anything and is, therefore, undetectable directly or indirectly by any sort of observation. We would be inclined to treat S as a paradigm of a sentence that is logically unconfirmable since we would contradict S if we offered a description of circumstances under which S might be confirmed. Now, as I have said, we are supposing that SP is a contemporary of ours who has made thousands upon thousands of correct predictions and never an incorrect one; and thus we have a very solid basis for giving full credence to anything he said. Let us then suppose that he asserts that S is true. There seems to be no reason to deny that in such a case S would have to be regarded as strongly verified by virtue of the fact that it has been asserted by the unique person who has proven himself, beyond reasonable doubt, to speak nothing but the truth.

If we were to accept this argument, however, then it is quite clear that the verification principle would have become completely useless. Few will want to deny that it is logically possible that such an SP could exist. It is also very easy to imagine that SP could claim S to be true, no matter what sentence S stands for (assuming S to be coherent). It follows that there are then no meaningless sentences at all, since every sentence would be verifiable *in principle*. We could always coherently describe a situation in which S would actually be confirmed: it is a situation in which SP claims S to be true.

It is worth pointing out that this objection is not to be met by once more claiming that what we have here is a content-independent implication since regardless of what we substitute for S it is true that if SP were to testify that S was true, we had the same reason to believe that S indeed was true. As we shall see shortly, this kind of consideration constitutes no obstacle to accepting as credible the testimony of a truthworthy informant. The real reason why this objection is entirely unfounded is that it does not in fact provide any basis for maintaining that it is logically possible that SP would assure us that S was true. Naturally, it is conceivable that he should do so in the sense that we can well picture him doing so, but for all we know this would be logically impossible. Given the definition of SP, it amounts to a contradiction to assert that he would testify that S was true (or that it was false) in case S was in fact meaningless. Thus unless we established first by some other means that S was definitely meaningful we are not in a position to insist that it is logically possible that SP should be able to tell us its truth value.

Section 3

The acquisition of justified belief

Let me conclude by considering a question that will bring us back to the heart of epistemology once more. There are all sorts of ways in which '$JBaS$' may be brought about. Referring again to a sentence discussed in the previous chapter where 'S_1' denoted 'Howard is a coward', clearly there is a very large variety of ways in which a may acquire an adequately justified belief that S_1 is true. a may witness any variety of behaviour in vastly different situations which he interprets as manifestations of cowardice on Howard's part and which would from an objective point of view be correctly interpreted. In addition, however, a's belief that S_1 could be fully justified even if he himself has no direct evidence to support it. For example, his friend Fred who has proven to be a most reliable truthful person informs a that he knows for sure that Howard is a coward.

   Now one may wonder: why is there such a difference between the way justified belief can be acquired on the one hand and the way meaningfulness is established or understanding be obtained on the other? Let us consider the issue of the acquisition of a partial understanding we have examined in the previous chapter. It seemed to us self-evident that on the truth-condition analysis of understanding my knowledge of the relevance of such indirect conditions as information obtained from authority is completely worthless. Recall that we postulated a situation in which I had no idea what the word 'coward' stood for and hence had no clue whatever as to the meaning of S_1:

I have however a friend Fred who has proven himself to be a most reliably truthful person. I know therefore that if Fred should assert that S_1 was true then S_1 must be true ... it would seem absurd to claim that my knowledge of this contributes in the slightest to my understanding of S_1.

Thus what seems puzzling is that in the case of 'understanding' and 'meaningfulness' the logical relation between the relevant elements must be content-dependent while in the context of 'justified belief' there is no such requirement. However a brief reflection will reveal an important difference between the two cases. This difference is basically rooted in the fact that in one case we have a reliable informant *actually* telling us that S_1 *is* true while in the other we merely claim to know what *would* be the case if such an informant *were* to tell us that S_1 was true.

Let me explain this in somewhat greater detail. When our objective is established that a's belief that S_1, is rationally warranted, i.e. that $JBaS_1$, then of course we may take it that a understands what S_1 stands for and what he needs is adequate evidence that S_1 is true. Now Fred vouching for the truth of S_1 provides the required evidence. It would be a mistake to think that a's conclusion that S_1 was credible has been arrived at through an inconsequential kind of inference. For surely it would be wrong to claim that regardless of what S_1 stood for, Fred would testify that it was true. The fact that Fred is a fully reliable and truthful person decidedly implies that it is only because S_1 stands specifically for the statement it happens to stand for by the conventions of our language that he assures us of its veracity, and if it stood for any of the contraries of that statement he would insist it was false. On the other hand, in order to secure the understanding of a sentence what is required is a knowledge not of the truth *value* of that sentence but merely of its truth *conditions*. In that context therefore we may assert that *if* Fred should certify S_1 to be true then that *would* constitute adequate evidence for it being so. This conditional assertion is universally true for any imaginable S_1: for if S_1 expressed a false statement or expressed no statement at all the antecendent of our conditional would be false. Given Fred's reliability we may rest assured that he would not certify a sentence to express a true statement if it did not do so.

Notes

INTRODUCTION

1 To be precise, we shall not be dealing with expressions in which there is quantification of the *subject* of the sentence said to be known or believed.

CHAPTER ONE

1 *See* Hocutt [1], p. 435.
2 Levy [1], p. 00.
3 I owe this point to John Pollock.
4 *See* Steiner [1].
5 *See* Ginet [2].

CHAPTER TWO

1 *See* Alston [1].
2 *See* Chapter 5 of Ryle [1].
3 *See* Hocutt [1].
4 MacIntosh [1].

CHAPTER THREE

1 Denbigh [1].
2 Carrier [1], p. 144.
3 Haack [2].
4 Since $(p) \diamond Bap$ and $(p) \diamond Ba \sim p$ say just the same thing.
5 Feldman [1], p. 267.
6 Stove [1], p. 47.
7 Mott [1].
8 Haack [1], p. 00.
9 The material implication, $\supset$, is used in (α) in preference to logical implication ($\rightarrow$). Thus (ϕ) denies the existence of a justification which would, simply as a matter of fact, guarantee truth.
10 *See* Lenzen [1].
11 Moore [1], p. 187.
12 Teller [1].

CHAPTER FOUR

1 *See* Griffin and Harton [1].
2 Ibid., p. 25.
3 Lehrer [1].
4 Ibid., p. 351.
5 Hilpinen [3].

CHAPTER FIVE

1 *See* Kahneman and Tversky [1].
2 *See* Blyth [1] and Blyth [2].
3 *See* Tlumak and Shuger [1].
4 *See* Quinn [1], p. 62.
5 *See* Sorensen [1] and Chisholm and Kiem [1].
6 Sorensen [1], p. 15.
7 Ginet [3], p. 35.

CHAPTER SIX

1 *See* Chisholm [1].
2 *Eap* means 'p is justified for a'.
3 *See* al-Hibri [1].
4 Decow [1].
5 For example, if $Pr(A) = n - \varepsilon$, then $Pr(B/A)$ need not be greater than $n^2/n - \varepsilon$ for their product to be n^2 (which is additionally, the value of the product on the left hand side of (CA')).
6 *See* Tomberlin [1].
7 In von Wright [2].
8 von Wright [2], p. 119.
9 Chellas [1], p. 201.
10 Conee [1].
11 In Glymour [1].
12 Levy [1].
13 von Kutschera [1].
14 *See* al-Hibri [1] and Hensson [1].
15 Hensson [1], p. 146.
16 *See* von Wright [1] and Stenius [1].
17 von Wright [3], p. 30.
18 Ibid., p. 29.
19 In Girill [1], pp. 151–2.

CHAPTER SEVEN

1 Ginet [1], p. 24.
2 Quine [1], p. 88.

3 Glymour [1], pp. 35–6.
4 *See* Schlesinger [1], pp. 140–4.

CHAPTER EIGHT

1 Harrison [1], p. 67.
2 Dummett [1], p. 126.
3 *See* Swinburne [1].
4 Mackie [1], pp. 90–2.
5 Ibid., p. 91.
6 Schlesinger [2], p. 146.
7 *See* Ayer [1], p. 00.
8 Berlin [1].
9 Glymour [1], p. 33.

Bibliography

al-Hibri, Aziza [1] *Deontic Logic* (Washington: University Press of America, 1978)

Alston, William P [1] Varieties of Privileged Access, *American Philosophical Quarterly* 8 (1971)

Ayer, A J [1] *Language, Truth and Logic* (New York: Dover, 1946)

Berlin, I [1] Verification, *Proceedings of the Aristotelian Society* 39 (1938-9)

Blyth, Colin R [1] On Simpson's Paradox and the Sure-Things Principle, *Journal of the American Statistical Association* 67 (1972)

Carrier, L S [1] Scepticism Made Certain, *Journal of Philosophy* 71 (1974)

Chellas, B F [1] *Modal Logic* (Cambridge: Cambridge University Press, 1980)

Chisholm, R [1] The Ethics of Requirement, *American Philosophical Quarterly* 1 1964)

—— and Kiem, R G [1] A system of Epistemic Logic, *Ratio* 14 (1972)

Conee, Earl [1] Against Moral Dilemmas, *Philosophical Review* 91 (1982)

Decow, J W [1] Conditional Obligation and Counterfactuals, *Journal of Philosophical Logic* 10 (1981)

Denbigh, K G [1] *An Inventive Universe* (New York: George Braziller, 1975)

Dummett, M [1] What is a Theory of Meaning? (II), in Evans and McDowell [1]

Evans, G and McDowell, J [1] *Truth and Meaning* (Oxford: Oxford University Press, 1976)

Feldman, Richard [1] Fallibilism and Knowing that One Knows, *Philosophical Review* 90 (1981)

Ginet, Carl [1] *Knowledge, Perception and Memory* (Dordrecht: D Reidel, 1975)

—— [2] Knowing Less By Knowing More, *Midwest Studies in Philosophy* 5 (1980)

—— [3] Justification of Belief, in Ginet and Shoemaker [1]

—— and Shoemaker, S (eds) [1] *Knowledge and Mind* (Oxford: Oxford University Press, 1982)

Girill, T R [1] On the Comparison of Inductive Support with Deontic Requirements, *Grazer Philosophische Studien* 9 (1979)

Griffin, N and Harton, M [1] Sceptical Arguments, *Philosophical Quarterly* 31 (1981)

Guttenplan, S [1] *Mind and Language* (Oxford: Oxford University Press, 1975)

Haack, Susan [1] *Philosophy of Logics* (Cambridge: Cambridge University Press, 1978)

―― [2] Fallibilism and Necessity, *Synthese* **41** (1979)

Hensson, Bengt [1] An Analysis of Some Deontic Logics, in Hilpinen [1]

Harrison, B [1] *An Introduction to the Philosophy of Language* (New York: St Martin's Press, 1979)

Hilpinen, R (ed) [1] *Deontic Logic: Introductory and Systematic Readings* (Dordrecht: D Reidel, 1971)

―― (ed) [2] *New Studies in Deontic Logic* (Dordrecht: D Reidel, 1981)

―― [3] Scepticism and Justification, *Synthese* **58** (1983)

Hocutt, Max O [1] Is Epistemic Logic Possible? *Notre Dame Journal of Formal Logic* **13** (1972)

Kahneman, and **Tversky,** [2] Subjective Probability: A Judgment of Representativeness, *Cognitive Psychology* **3** (1972)

Lehrer, Keith [1] Why Not Scepticism? in Pappas and Swain [1]

Lenk, H (ed) [1] *Normen Logik: Grundprobleme der deontische Logik* (Munich: Pullach, 1974)

Lenzen, W [1] Recent Work in Epistemic Logic, *Acta Philosophica Fennica* **30** (19)

Levy, Stephen [1] Do You Know Everything You Know? *Canadian Journal of Philosophy* **9** (1979)

MacIntosh, J J [1] The Logic of Privileged Access, *Australasian Journal of Philosophy* **61** (1983)

Mackie, J L [1] Truth and Verifiability, *Analysis* **40** (1980)

Moore, G E [1] *Commonplace Books* (London: George Allan and Unwin, 1962)

Mott, P L [1] Haack and Fallibilism, *Analysis* **40** (1980)

Pappas, G S and **Swain, M** (eds) [1] *Essays on Knowledge and Justification* (Ithaca: Cornell University Press, 1978)

Quine, W V [1] Mind and Verbal Disposition, in Guttenplan [1]

Ryle, Gilbert [1] *The Concept of Mind* (London: Hutchinson, 1949)

Schlesinger, G [1] *Metaphysics: Methods and Problems* (Oxford: Basil Blackwell, 1980)

―― [2] *Aspects of Time* (Indianapolis: Hackett, 1983)

Sorensen, R A [1] Subjective Probability and Indifference, *Analysis* **43** (1983)

Steiner, Mark [1] Cartesian Scepticism and Epistemic Logic, *Analysis* **39** (1979)

Stenius, E [1] Ross's Paradox and Well-Formed Codices, *Theoria* (1982)

Stove, David [1] *Popper and After* (Oxford: Pergamon, 1982)

Swinburne, R (ed) [1] *Space, Time and Causality* (Dordrecht: D Reidel, 1983)

Teller, Paul [1] Epistemic Possibility, *Philosophia* **2** (1972)

Tlumark, J and **Shuger, S**   [1] The Hardiness of Knowledge, *American Philosophical Quarterly* **18** (1981)

Tomberlin, J   [1] Contrary to Duty Imperatives and Conditional Obligation, *Nous* **15** (1981)

von Kutschera, F   [1] Normative Preferenzen und bedingte Gebote, in Lenz [1]

von Wright, G H   [1] An Essay in Deontic Logic and the General Theory of Action, *Acta Philosophica Fennica* **21** (1968)

——— [2] A New System of Deontic Logic, in Hilpinen [1]

——— [3] On the Logic of Norms and Actions, in Hilpinen [2]

Quinn, Philip   [1] Some Epistemic Implications of 'Crucial Experiments', *Studies in History and Philosophy of Science* **5** (1974)

Subject Index